# THE BOOK
## OF
## PRAISE

*Mark Van Doren*
*and*
*Maurice Samuel*

# THE BOOK
# OF
# PRAISE

*Dialogues on the Psalms*

EDITED AND ANNOTATED BY
Edith Samuel

*The John Day Company*
*New York*

Designed by Stanley S. Drate

Manufactured in the United States of America

Library of Congress Cataloging in Publication Data

Van Doren, Mark, 1894–1972.
   The book of praise.

   1. Bible. O.T. Psalms—Criticism, interpretation,
etc.   I. Samuel, Maurice, 1895–1972.   II. Samuel,
Edith, ed.   III. Title.
BS1430.2.V36   1974      223'.2'077      74–9362
ISBN 0–381–98271–8

10 9 8 7 6 5 4 3 2 1

# ACKNOWLEDGMENTS

All biblical quotations used in the dialogues, unless otherwise identified, are reprinted by permission of The Jewish Publication Society of America from *The Holy Scriptures,* English translation, copyright © 1917, 1955.

Excerpt on page 7 reprinted by permission of Monsignor Joseph B. Frey from *My Daily Psalm: The Book of Psalms Arranged for Each Day of the Week,* edited by Monsignor Joseph B. Frey, Confraternity of the Precious Blood, New York.

Excerpt on page 15 preprinted by permission of Harcourt Brace Javanovich, Inc., from *Chicago Poems,* copyright © 1916, by Holt, Rhinehart and Winston, copyright 1944, by Carl Sandburg.

Excerpt on page 22 from *Collected Poems* by Ralph Hodgson, copyright © 1958, 1961, by Ralph Hodgson, reprinted by permission of Mrs. R. Hodgson; Macmillan, London and Basingstoke; the Macmillan Company of Canada Limited; and Macmillan Publishing Company, Inc., New York.

Excerpt on page 231 from *Heritage of Music* by Judith Kaplan Eisenstein, copyright © 1972, by Union of American Hebrew Congregations, quoted by permission of the publisher; Union of American Hebrew Congregations, New York.

Excerpts on pages 233, 241, and 243 reprinted by permission of The Jewish Publication Society of America from *The Torah: The Five Books of Moses.* A New Translation of the Holy Scriptures, According to the Masoretic Text, copyright © 1962.

Excerpts on pages 237, 240, 242, 249, 251 and 255 reprinted by permission of Rabbi Gershon Hadas from *The Book of Psalms for the Modern*

# CONTENTS

## XIII OF HUMILITY AND PRAISE

*Must we "sow in tears" in order "to reap in joy"?—Creative frustration—Some views of Shakespeare—"Hallelujah, I'm alive!"—Giving praise where praise is due—On being "nice" to people—The spontaneity of praise in the psalms—"A man has to praise God!"—Fear and trembling in the psalms—A little lower than God Himself—The whole world as a praise of God—Where is our literature of astonishment?—Praising the unpraiseworthy— Creative misunderstandings and misreadings—Riding an iambic pentameter*

## XIV ALL THE GLORY OF THE UNIVERSE

*The great Hallels—The creatures of the earth in Psalm 104— Leviathan and the great feast in the world-to-come—Man the unknown in Psalm 139—Teleology as an offensive word today— $H_2O$—Purpose in the universe—The macrocosmic and the microcosmic—Psalms 139 and 148 contrasted—The music of the spheres—The peepers in springtime—"If I'm not around, there ain't nothin'!"—A song is a song—His glory is His glory— Shakespeare a delusion?—"Put not your trust in princes"—Infinitudes of interpretations—The voices of all living things praising Him*

# ABOUT
# *The Book of Praise:*
# A FOREWORD

I

This is the second book of dialogues on the Bible between Mark Van Doren, Pulitzer Prize poet, and Maurice Samuel, Jewish author and lecturer, that I have retrieved out of the air.

The first—*In the Beginning, Love,* published in 1973—recaptured in print the spoken exchanges between the two master teachers on the general theme of love in the Bible. In this second book, I have set down their searching talks on the Book of Psalms, a book they regarded as poetry beyond poetry. Their sense of wonder before these marvelous human expressions never froze their lips: they were able to discover fresh words to open up the Book of Psalms for moderns and help them feel its incomparable beauty and strength.

The Hebrew name for the Book of Psalms is *Sefer Tehillim,* "Book of Praises." In their dialogues about the book, Mark Van Doren and Maurice Samuel found many additional phrases to characterize the psalms. For Mark, they were, among other things, "the greatest lyric poems in the world [whose] substance is deeper than the level of language." For Maurice, the Book of Psalms was, again among other things, "the intellectual book without intellectuality." This present book then may in a sense be read as *their* book of praise for the immortal *Book of Praises.*

2

In *In the Beginning, Love,* Mark Van Doren charmingly recalled the circumstances of his first meeting in 1952 with Maurice Samuel, who was my husband. The two were brought together originally to record a series of spontaneous, unrehearsed conversations on the Bible for "The Eternal Light" radio program of The Jewish Theological Seminary of America. This much acclaimed public service program of the National Broadcasting Company has now been on the air for many years, and is heard across the country. Their first series of dialogues, broadcast in the summer of 1953, was warmly received. Subsequently, every summer thereafter, the two came together for their unique dialogues on some aspect of the Bible. Their last series went out on the air in the summer of 1972, the year that Maurice and later Mark died.

3

Both men loved the Bible, and in almost twenty sum-
mers of wide-ranging conversations about it, never
once did they run out of ideas, humor, anecdotes,
information, insights, elucidations, quotations or zest
for their subject. Neither regarded himself as a Bible
"specialist" in the formal, technical sense. Mark Van
Doren taught the Bible as literature for a decade in a
famous English course he gave at Columbia University; he wrote some captivating poetry and essays on
biblical themes. Maurice lectured on and off about
certain aspects of the Bible for some fifty years, and he,
too, wrote his own enchanting embroideries of biblical characters and themes. Both men respectfully
tipped their hats, so to speak, to the Bible scholars—
the archeologists, the comparative religionists, the tex-
tual analysts, etc.—and imperturbably went their own
way. The artifacts and the raw details of Bible structure—did such-and-such Hebrew verse, for instance,
relate to thus-and-thus in the Akkadian? was this-and-
this chapter misnumbered in a biblical book?—were
interesting, to be sure, but not their thing. As literary
men of imagination, creativity and style, their concern
was with meaning and communication. What was the
*sense* of the words? What was their special quality, and
how did they affect the spirit? Why did the men and
women of the Bible—and for Maurice and Mark, they
were very real flesh-and-blood people—do this, say
that? In all of their exchanges, Mark and Maurice were
trying to uncover the layers of wisdom, beauty, and
truth in the Bible, for themselves as much as for others.

4

The Book of Psalms is the longest book in the Bible, and next to the Book of Genesis, probably the best known and most universally popular. It became the basis for the Jewish liturgy, and for the Christian as well; and outside the church and the synagogue, countless millions have been reading, reciting, and singing the psalms for twenty-five hundred years and possibly longer. In Judaism to this day, there are *hevrot tehillim,* societies of reciters of psalms, who know the entire Hebrew book by heart. Today there are two groups who daily go to the Western Wall in Jerusalem and chant the book from beginning to end. During the Yom Kippur War of October 1973, thousands of copies of *Sefer Tehillim* were distributed to Israeli troops at the front. The influence of the Book of Psalms upon the music, art and literature of the Western world is, as the encyclopedias put it, "incalculable." One cannot even begin to guess at the immeasurable impact of this book upon generation after generation of people who turned to it—in the original Hebrew or in translation into virtually every language known to man—in times of calamity or rejoicing, of despair or of hope, of piercing sorrow or boundless joy; in moments of personal fear, pain, remorse, loneliness, longing, and also of gladness, gratitude, and serene contemplation. The Book of Psalms is a religious book, and as Maurice and Mark point out, it is addressed to God; yet unbelievers also read it, quote it, and treasure it.

Against this background, Mark and Maurice began their conversations by trying to discover why the psalms exert such profound power on the human spirit. They examined the language and the moods of the psalms, speculated upon the identity (or identities) of the Psalmist, then went on to consider some of the marvelous passages in several dozen psalms. In their fourteen dialogues, they could not, of course, examine all of the 150 psalms in the book; but what they had to say about those examples they chose was—and is— enough to send anyone back to the book.

As the reader will learn, in the course of commenting on the psalms, Maurice and Mark roamed happily through world literature—Browning, Shakespeare, Thoreau, I. L. Peretz, Joyce, Socrates, Sandburg—and, as was their wont, touched on innumerable human concerns: man's insolence toward nature, sons and fathers, the power of the tongue, self-righteousness, the evil man, the compulsion to praise, the language of poetry, the guilt complex, the wonder of the universe. These "digressions" were unplanned: one mind sparked the other, and out flowed the stored wisdom, wit, and experience.

5

In editing these dialogues, I have used the blue pencil as sparingly as possible to allow the original charm and grace, the digressions and occasionally the differences between the two, to come through. I have retained the signs of laughter, those sudden bursts that punctuated all the exchanges between the two, on or off the air. Wherever necessary, I have deleted half-sentences, rounded off incompleted quotations, and excised dangling ideas. Every now and then, one or the other would raise a question that was overlooked in the rush of talk. The reader will have to search out the answers himself, as both men would have liked. To assist the reader—indeed, to encourage him to go beyond the immediate discussion and add his own observations—I have placed the biblical references in the margins. For good measure, I have appended my own personal notes. They will have little interest for the scholar, but I offer them cheerfully to the general reader.

The edition of the Book of Psalms used in the dialogues was the 1917 English translation of The Holy Scriptures published by The Jewish Publication Society of Philadelphia. All the biblical quotations here, unless otherwise identified, come from that source. It is very close to the superb King James Version, which both men regarded as the most beautiful translation in the English language. New translations of the psalms have been appearing over the years. Some readers may find it rewarding, as I did, to look up variant readings of favorite passages. I was especially struck by the simplicity and clarity of *The Book of Psalms for the Modern Reader* by our dear friend, Rabbi Gershon Hadas of Kansas City, Missouri. Other translations consulted include the Revised Standard Version, an ecumenical edition published in 1973; and the 1972 translation of the Book of Psalms by The Jewish Publication Society of America. Some of the renditions in the latter work are so different from what many of us memorized in childhood as to be absolutely startling.

## 6

I want to express my sincere thanks to The Jewish Theological Seminary of America and the National Broadcasting Company for their kindness in waiving their rights in this undertaking. It was under their aegis that Mark Van Doren and Maurice Samuel were able to come together year after year for their inimitable conversations. Our good friend, Mr. Milton E. Krents, director of radio and TV for the Seminary, who brought the two together in 1952, had the responsibility for arranging another and yet another new series of dialogues every year for nearly two decades. It was a task he always approached with enormous relish and delight.

Dr. Ben Zion Bokser, spiritual leader of the Forest Hills Jewish Center and program editor of "The Eternal Light," has once again been kind enough to review the text of the dialogues before publication. I am deeply grateful to him. Dorothy Van Doren has also reviewed the text. Her efforts, like my own, have been a labor of love.

I wish finally to thank the numerous friends— many of them strangers—who took the trouble to write me, after reading *In the Beginning, Love.* They voiced gratitude to me for retrieving the dialogues of the two unseen but warmly welcomed guests in their homes every summer via radio; and they asked for more. No thanks are due me. It has been *my* joy to share with them the words of their teachers and my own.

EDITH SAMUEL

# I

# "THE BOOK
# OF GOD"

SAMUEL:   We've taken on a most formidable task, Mark—a discussion of the Book of Psalms. It's formidable not only because this is the longest book in the Bible, but also because, to me, it is the heaviest with meaning. In a sense—if one may so put it—it is the backbone of the Bible. I can no more conceive of the Bible without a Book of Psalms than *Hamlet,* as the saying goes, without the Prince of Denmark.

VAN DOREN:   There are people, I dare say, who would suppose that the Book of Psalms was a very simple thing to talk about. They'd say that it's only a collection of short poems—all of them alike!

SAMUEL:   Now that you mention it, Mark, I'll add another reason to my list of "formidables"—the tremendous diversity in the Book of Psalms. But before we get into details, let me ask you: What is it that has given these psalms their peculiar hold upon the whole of the Western religious world? What lifts this book out of even the very lofty, the very exalted material which constitutes the rest of the Bible? What gives this book its outstanding and unforgettable power?

VAN DOREN: I could answer in many ways, and I probably shall before we're finished. But my first answer, I think, had better be this: the subject of the Book of Psalms is God. Now, the subject of *every* book of the Bible is God. He is present in every book; He is basic, central, to it. And yet in Psalms, somehow, He is *more* present than ever. He is what all the psalms are dealing with. They are all addresses to Him; or they are all praises and celebrations of Him; or they are all descriptions of Him, or statements of the great things He has done. Somehow or other, this is the Book of God. I say that quite simply. Do you think I exaggerate?

SAMUEL: No, you don't exaggerate at all. Let me put it another way. There are certain parts of the Bible where God, as it were, retreats from the scene, and the action takes place among men. He isn't forgotten, but in a sense, He has withdrawn—for example, in the struggles of men, and in certain narrative portions. In the Book of Esther, He isn't mentioned at all! But you're perfectly right in saying that here in the psalms, He is implicit and immanent in every verse. You can't pick up a psalm and say to yourself: "Well, for a moment, I'm going to rest myself from the tremendous pressure of His presence." All the time, He is about you like a cloud. You're moving *in Him* all the time!

VAN DOREN: That's a wonderful statement, Maurice. I like the word "immanent" particularly. He "dwells" in this book, because of course "dwells in" is what "immanent" means. His presence always "presses" upon us. Sometimes His presence is joyful; sometimes it is not joyful, because there is a sense that He has been forgotten, or perhaps for a while has ceased to have attended to men's concerns; but He always comes back again. The concerns of men, of course, are a subject here, too; Psalms *is* a book spoken by men, sung by men. The book is not spoken by God; it is spoken *to* God. I would say that all the concerns of men that I can imagine are somehow here.

SAMUEL: What is remarkable about the Book of Psalms is that in spite of this overwhelming omnipresence, this ubiquity of God, there is more variety in this one book than in any other book in the Bible. The moods vary—the moods in which God is approached, or apprehended, or feared. Or sometimes, as you intimated, it is His absence that is felt: a man suddenly feels that he's been abandoned by God. And, of course, then God is present most of all.

VAN DOREN: "My God, my God, why hast Thou forsaken me?" PSALM 22:2

SAMUEL: Yes, in the midst of what you would imagine to be this crushing uniformity, there is more play of color and emotion than in any other single book of the Bible.

VAN DOREN: The existence of God is never in the slightest degree doubted. No speaker of any of these poems is ever endeavoring to prove the existence of God. God's existence is assumed (and "assumed" is a rather weak word here when His dimensions are so immense). But His presence, His immanence, can always be believed. We sometimes in our world are so far from that view that it isn't funny. You're familiar with the statement one hears repeated from time to time nowadays, that men "made" God—men "invented" or "conceived" Him—and that they somehow keep Him alive. Well, no one of the Jews who had anything to do with this book would have been able to make any sense out of that at all, because it was so natural for him to understand that God made *him* and that God made *all* men.

SAMUEL: This attitude of men imputing to others the power to create God—as though they weren't the creatures of God, but rather, they project God—this is a complete misunderstanding of what the Bible is about, and particularly of what the Book of Psalms is about. This *is* "God-intoxicated man" in the Book of Psalms. Now, if we carry this a bit further: intoxication has its various stages down to the point of stupor, where a man forgets that there is God, even though he is—so to speak—drenched with God. But to make God the essential theme of the Book of

Psalms is a necessary preliminary to a discussion of it.

VAN DOREN: By all means. And we must remember, too, how easy it was for the Jews, creating this book, to think of God as greater not only than themselves, but greater than any other creature, greater than the whole world. He had created the world, and that meant that He existed before it. He exists independently of it; and although the psalms make much use of the world, the parts of it and the objects in it, as poetry always must (since it has to have a language, and the language must refer to things that men know), yet there is never any forgetting that God is eternal. He was there before He formed the mountains and the earth, as the Psalmist says, and He is God now, "from everlasting to everlasting."                    PSALM 90:2

SAMUEL: Yes, He was, and He *is*. Toward the end of the book, we'll come across a great burst of lyrical praise expressing His presence everywhere, and throughout all time—phrases like: "If I take the wings of the morning, And dwell in the uttermost parts of the sea; If I ascend up into heaven, Thou art there; . . ." This feeling of the omnipresence of God has pursued Jews, particularly the Jewish mystics, down into modern times. I wonder, Mark, if you know the famous "Thou" song of the great Hasidic rabbi, Levi Yitzhak of Berditchev?[1] It was sung originally in Yiddish, with some Hebrew words and phrases mixed in. The song has here and there been translated into English.

PSALM
139:9, 8

VAN DOREN:   Oh yes, I've heard about it.

SAMUEL:   A good part of it consists of excla-
mations: "Thou! Where I go—Thou! East, Thou!
West, Thou! North, Thou! South, Thou! Everywhere
—Thou!" This is something which issues from the
psalmodic mood: man is incapable of escaping from
Him, even in his most desperate moments. And of
course, as we examine the psalms, we're going to come
across not only supplication and confession, but despair and despondency as well. We're going to delve
into various other themes, too. The opening statement
you made is a good one, and basic to all our talks: the
Book of Psalms is immersed in God Himself.

VAN DOREN:   I must make a confession at this
point, Maurice. When we decided upon this subject
for our conversations, I was very happy at the prospect
of talking about the psalms, but I had no conception
at that moment of their variety. I knew they were not
monotonous; I knew they contained a variety of poetic
power—that is, different images and ideas were found
and exploited in all of them. But I didn't know or
remember what a range of subject matter there was in
the book, how many concerns and needs of men were
dealt with. To me, it was a revelation to reread the
Book of Psalms!

SAMUEL:   I think that what takes place with all
of us—and probably took place with you—is this: every time one reads the Book of Psalms particularly,
one seems to feel, "I didn't see that before"—*even if
one did!* It comes over you with such a renewed impact

that all the former impressions are obliterated, and it's re-created for you on the spot. I think *that,* rather, is the substance of your experience.

VAN DOREN: Exactly! That was why I was so excited when I came upon a statement about the psalms which I found as a preface to an edition of them that I wanted to take with me recently on a plane trip, because all the time I've been preparing to discuss the psalms with you, I've been reading them now and then, here and there. It isn't the kind of reading you can do all at once. You've got to return to it, to live with it, in that sense. This little book had these re-marks:

> *The Book of Psalms is for all times, all circumstances, and all needs. It is for everybody. The psalms rhyme with every mood of man. No longing of the soul, no craving of the mind, no bodily want, exists which cannot be expressed in the sublime phrases of the psalms. Prayers in the morning, during the day for guidance in work, of repentance for sin, of thanksgiving and adoration; prayers for loved ones, and for all the world, prayers in the evening, prayers in time of trouble or sickness, and countless others are to be found in the psalms. It is the perfect prayer book.*[2]

SAMUEL: That's a very beautiful statement.

VAN DOREN: It moved me because it chimed so perfectly with experiences I'd been having.

SAMUEL: Notice, by the way, we use the word "psalms." Originally, that was a neutral word; *psalmos* in Greek was simply "playing on a musical instrument." Now in Hebrew, this book is called *Sefer*

*Tehillim,* the "Book of Praises." The word *tehillim* is connected with the Hebrew word *hallel,* "praise," from which we get the word "hallelujah."[3]

VAN DOREN: Which means "praise God."

SAMUEL: *Hallelu,* "praise ye," and *Yah* or *Jah,* "the Lord." We've imposed on the neutral word "psalm" all the meaning, the colorfulness, and all the profundity of emotion which is contained in the book. But Mark, I'm going to give this conversation a special turn just now because I'm anxious to have your views on the poetical structure of the psalms. The book is "literature" in the highest sense, and therefore, the *modes* as well as the moods in which the Psalmist expresses himself must have for you a special appeal; and if I may so put it without being misunderstood, a *technical* appeal. There's an ingenuity in the psalms which was created by the Psalmist in giving vent to his various moods. The ingenuity isn't a deliberate effort, but rather, it comes from the force of the man's feelings. Mark, as a poet yourself, how would you describe the particular tonality of the poetical spirit of the psalms?

VAN DOREN: I agree with some of the commentators whom I've been reading, who have said that the psalms are not properly understood until they are understood as poems. One will understand them as poems are to be understood—that is to say, not always in terms of a statement or a proposition that could just as well be made in prose, or in a relaxed and neutral voice, but something that must be said in this very special way. By "special way," I might mean something that anyone notices as he begins to read the psalms, this thing often called "parallelism." The Psalmist has the habit of saying a thing, and then immediately saying it again, with a little difference, a little variation. This is something like the variation that takes place in music. You know, one reason that music is so charming to us—although we may not know this —is that we hear a phrase, and then we hear it again, with inversion, with additions, or subtractions, or in different time, or something of that sort. Repetition is of the essence of poetic speech; I'm not merely referring to the refrain, or to rhyme, but to something that keeps coming, keeps coming. There it is again! It rolls over us, as waves do. Anyone notices this in all the lyric portions of the Bible, but it is particularly apparent here in the Book of Psalms. The very first psalm begins by saying the same thing twice:

*Happy is the man that hath not walked in the counsel of the* PSALM 1:1
   *wicked,*
*Nor stood in the way of sinners, . . .*

SAMUEL: "Stood in the way of sinners," Mark, might be misunderstood by some people to mean that the man has *obstructed* the sinners. This possibility of misunderstanding is one of the reasons why translations must be revised from time to time. "Stood in the way of sinners" means "loitered along" with them.

VAN DOREN: Yes, "stood where sinners are." Now this repetition comes again, almost immediately, in the second verse:

PSALM 1:2            *But his delight is in the law of the Lord;*
                         *And in His law doth he meditate day and night.*

Now there it is: it's said again, of course, with additions. Because if his delight is in the law, why then *of course* he meditates in it day and night, but it is nevertheless said.

SAMUEL: Wait a minute, Mark! "Delight in the law, meditate in it day and night:" what I see there as a very particular point that's being established is—you must not delight in this thing *occasionally.* That is, don't go to it when you just feel some aesthetic impulse, and say, "Oh, isn't that a nice passage! Isn't that a nice phrase!" This is something which must be your constant companion. So that the repetition there isn't merely a repetition; it is also a reinforcement. This technique of repetition in the Bible is called "dittology." It's as though a man were speaking across mountaintops and the voice rolled back to him; but when it came back, it had been altered by some power over there, and it added to what he said.

VAN DOREN: Oh, by all means! I don't mean mere repetition; I mean repetition—as I said in the case of music—with addition. It is everywhere. Here's another example:

PSALM 38:2         *O Lord, rebuke me not in Thine anger,*
                      *Neither chasten me in Thy wrath.*

The second line is almost exactly the same as the first, except "chasten" adds something to "rebuke" there, I should say.

SAMUEL:   Or you'll get passages like these:

> *Smoother than cream were the speeches of his mouth,*
> *But his heart was war;*
> *His words were softer than oil,*
> *Yet were they keen-edged swords.*

PSALM
55:22

Here you don't need anything more than this launching of the idea, and its recoil upon you with the variation, and the deepening which comes with the variation. Now here is the Psalmist using repetition in another way:

> *I have not sat with men of falsehood;*
> *Neither will I go in with dissemblers.*
> *I hate the gatherings of evil-doers,*
> *And will not sit with the wicked.*

PSALM
26:4–5

In a sense, this is the very opposite of being repetitious. Sometimes a person repeats himself helplessly; and sometimes he envelops his old meaning in a new form, and gives you an insight you didn't have before. The latter can't properly be called "repeating."

VAN DOREN:   Oh, by all means! I didn't mean for a second that repetition here was anything weak. It is of the utmost strength. For instance, in the great Psalm 19, which may very well be the greatest of them all:

> *The law of the Lord is perfect, restoring the soul;*
> *The testimony of the Lord is sure, making wise the simple.*
> *The precepts of the Lord are right, rejoicing the heart;*
> *The commandment of the Lord is pure, enlightening the eyes.*
> *The fear of the Lord is clean, enduring for ever;*
> *The ordinances of the Lord are true, they are righteous altogether; . . .*

PSALM
19:8–10

There's a progression—a very definite progression; and yet somehow, a form has been set up, and the interest of the listener or the reader is at least double. His interest is in recognizing something that happens again, but also in recognizing something new, when it comes. This, by the way, is something that I think you tend to get in any great utterance of any kind, anywhere.

SAMUEL: Some people think that rhyme is essential to poetry, Mark. I was just thinking of that phrase of Milton's, "the jingling sound of like endings."[4] He speaks with contempt of the device of rhyme, although he himself made great use of it.

VAN DOREN: He was a great rhymer!

SAMUEL: Yes, his *Lycidas* and *Il Penseroso* and *L'Allegro* are very ingeniously rhymed. Nevertheless, for his greatest utterance—*Paradise Lost* and *Paradise Regained*—he went to the stateliness of unrhymed verse, the pentameter. As you've been explicating this matter, it occurs to me that perhaps it's true: the greatest verse *is* unrhymed. But beyond that, when you've escaped from the kind of rhythm which is constituted by rhyme, you've moved onto a higher stage, where the rhythm is constituted by the rhythm of the words themselves, unrhymed. You go a step higher when your rhythm is constituted purely by *ideas,* and not even by blank verse. Thus, perhaps this last kind is the highest form of poetry.

VAN DOREN: And of course, that might be one of the reasons why these psalms are the greatest of all lyric poems—because I think they *are* the greatest lyric poems in the world; they are more than that, too. Another reason might be that their substance is deeper than the level of language. You do not have to know Hebrew perfectly to get the essence of the psalms, because it comes to you, if in nothing else, in these parallelisms of which we've spoken. They are not rhyme, no trick of speech, no mere cleverness of the tongue; the essence of the psalms is an activity of the mind and of the soul that keeps the subject always rich and growing.

SAMUEL: Mark, have you ever read any of your poetry translated into another language?

VAN DOREN: Yes, I have—a few times.

SAMUEL: And how has it felt?

VAN DOREN: To tell the truth, I have never recognized it!

*(laughter)*

SAMUEL: What you've just said is perfectly true: great poetry somehow is bound to come through, and yet there is some atmospheric effect which has to get lost. Now, I don't know Hebrew perfectly; I read it well enough to get something in it that is absent even from that magnificent King James Version we have in English. Take a phrase in Psalms like, "Keep me as the   PSALM 17:8

apple of the eye." In another place in the Bible, the
DEUT. expression is "apple of His eye." That's a very beauti-
32: 10 ful phrase in English.[5] The Hebrew is equally beautiful, but it is quite different. "Apple of His eye" is *ishon
aino. Ishon* is "little man," and *aino* is "His eye."
When somebody says, "Guard me as the little man of
your eye!" he is really saying, "Guard *me!*" The "little
man" in *your* eye is *me!*

VAN DOREN:    Yes, the little man that I *see*
when I look in your eye!

SAMUEL:    That's right! When I look at you,
I'm there in your eye! The Hebrew phrase has a most
immediate and specific application. There's another
Hebrew phrase which is transposed in English translation. It's used in the Book of Genesis in connection
with the Patriarchs: Isaac, for example, "died . . . old
GEN. 35:29 and *s'va yomim,* full of days." What a tremendous
phrase! He was *crammed* with time! He couldn't eat
another minute, so he stopped eating time and he
died!

VAN DOREN *(laughing):*    He was packed with
time!

SAMUEL:    That's it! You couldn't get a pin-
point head of a fraction of a moment more into him!

VAN DOREN:    There's a suggestion also, I
think, that time had been richly spent. It hadn't been
wasted in him, or had just flowed through him: it had
all been dammed up in him, it had collected in him,

and had made him full. You know, speaking of these parallelisms, one finds them not only everywhere in the Bible, but also in other writings. I was amused the other day to be reading a poem by Carl Sandburg, our contemporary—his famous *Chicago*. Three little paragraphs of that poem—they're not stanzas because the poem is not metrical and not rhymed—begin like this (he's addressing the city of Chicago):

> *They tell me you are wicked, and I believe them; . . .*
> *And they tell me you are crooked, and I answer: . . .*
> *And they tell me you are brutal, and my reply is: . . .*

That's the same idea, isn't it?

SAMUEL: Yes. There is something else I want to ask you about, Mark, and we shall have to leave a discussion of it to next time; and that is the psalms— apart from their poetic power—as an assurance against the mechanistic view of life; the psalms as having the capacity to soften "the iron outline of the horizon," to use a phrase of Walter Pater's.[6] Now it happens that the psalms have an irresistible appeal even to those whom we might call a rationalist and an unbeliever. One might be tempted to explain, "That's because of the power of the poetry in the psalms." But that would be begging the question, because the psalms derive their power from that belief which is at the very base of them. It's a curious paradox. I've known many Jews here and in the State of Israel who call themselves "unbelievers," or "agnostics," or even "atheists," but they can't seem to get away from the Prophets and the psalms. They keep returning to the psalms with a certain satisfaction. You smile and say, "Now really, you

do *not* believe? What is this emotional response you
have to the psalms?" Now, this is the supremacy of
poetry that's beyond poetry, isn't it?

VAN DOREN:   I had an experience with my
students at Columbia University which resembles this
paradox you speak of. For ten years, I asked students
to read certain parts of the Bible and to discuss them
with me. After the fifth or the sixth meeting of the
class, or maybe in the second month of the class, I
would say: "Now gentlemen, many of you believe that
you do not believe in God. You know, you are young
men in the modern world, and if asked just on the
street, you might answer, 'No, I don't believe in God.'
But here we are reading the Book of Genesis. What
about *this* God? Do you believe that He is here?"
They all would smile; well, *of course* they did! How
could they doubt it? Maybe an hour later, in some
other context, they would begin the same old question. But to them *now,* it was not a question.

# II

# THE LANGUAGE OF THE PSALMS

SAMUEL: We closed last time, Mark, with a promise that we'd look into this matter of the psalms for "unbelievers" or for rationalists. Let's pursue that subject a little because it's one avenue of understanding the power of the psalms. I never cease to be amazed by the frequency with which men who call themselves unbelievers keep on using the psalms as emotional outlets. In one sense, you know, this is a kind of parasitism: they will use religious material as emotional nurture, but deny the source of the nourishment. However, that's by the way. The rationalist who looks upon the psalms as simply emotional material is quite false in his intellectual approach. I was often puzzled, for instance, by Blaise Pascal's approach to the question of belief. Here is this very deep believer making a gamble:

*Let us weigh the gain and the loss in wagering that God is.*
*Let us estimate these two chances. If you gain, you gain all;*
*if you lose, you lose nothing. Hesitate not, then, to wager that*
*He is.*[7]

"What have you got to lose by believing?" he asks—
as though it were such a simple matter! But, of course,
it wasn't and it isn't such a simple matter; and it should
be made clear to those who derive from literature of
this kind (if one may use the word "literature" without
further ado about it) a sustenance in life that there's
more involved merely than the emotional side. And
yet, I'm very anxious to probe through you—through
your poetic insight and knowledge—the actual technical side of the psalms. What is associated tech-
nically with this power of expression in the Book of
Psalms?

VAN DOREN:  You mean this power of expression which is the cause of the very effect that you
have been talking about, namely, the usableness of the
psalms, even by men who think they do not accept the
first principles that are somehow assumed in the book?
Well, I don't know that I like the word "technical" too
well. In English, we're in the unfortunate position of
being able to talk both about "art" and about "technique."

SAMUEL:  Yes, the word "art" sometimes
leads into "artful," just as the word "craft" leads into
the word "craftiness."

VAN DOREN:    Exactly! I've always envied the
Greeks because they had only one word for "art" and
that was *tekhnē*. They talked about the "art" of anything as the knowing how to do it, no matter what it
was. However, maybe I could take off from one word
that you used in your opening remarks: "intellectual."
In one sense, it seems to me, there's no intellectual
operation being conducted in the psalms. That doesn't
mean that there isn't a great deal of mind, a great deal
of intellect, if you please, being used; but it isn't being
used, as I said last time, to "prove" anything. It isn't
being used to establish that God exists, that He is
there, and that He is who and what He is. The Psalmist
is able to assume that; he *begins* there. And then the
operation of his mind is that of a poet's mind. It ex-
plores all the possibilities that follow upon this, all the
avenues that are open once belief exists. For instance,
the Psalmist's mind goes without any difficulty into
innumerable recesses of the created world to find images and objects with which to express his faith and his
feeling—not that the creation is anything more than
convenient for him. It is all about us, it is the thing that
we all know, the thing we—both the poet and the
listeners to the poet—live with. It is there, it is our
common life. And it has no ultimate value because the
Psalmist never forgets that God is greater than His
creation. One must not rest in the creation; and yet,
creation is the mine for his references and his images.
As I got ready to discuss the Book of Psalms with you,
I was very much interested in making a kind of list in
my mind of the images and the objects that are always
recurring in the psalms. They are the *body* of the work;
the *soul* of the work is something else. But poetry must

have body as well as soul. "Wings," for instance. Notice how that word recurs.

PSALM 17:8    SAMUEL:   "Hide me in the shadow of Thy wings."

PSALM 63:8    VAN DOREN:   ". . . in the shadow of Thy wings do I rejoice." Wings seem to fill the world of the Psalmist. It's as if there were nothing but a great pair or set of wings always there!

SAMUEL:   It's an image that keeps reappearing.

VAN DOREN:   And then the image of the high tower, the high rock, the solid rock—which God is. You will agree, I dare say, that time and time again, we are up against—so to speak—that rock, that unshakable, immovable mountain.

*e.g.,*
PSALMS
19:15 AND
144:1–2

SAMUEL:   Yes, "my Fortress," and "my Rock" are a favorite image with the Psalmist. Do you know, Mark, I almost went and counted the times that the word "heart" occurs in the psalms. It makes the effect of being innumerable. The Psalmist doesn't refer to the emotion alone: he refers to the agitation which it sets up in the body, and he uses that both for feeling and for intellection, to use a rather barbarous

PSALM 4:8
PSALM 7:11
PSALM 12:3

word: "Thou hast put gladness in my heart." Or in another instance, he speaks of "the upright in heart." Of deceivers, the Psalmist says they speak "with a double heart." Actually, we would say in English that they are "two-faced," or "double-faced"; but in the

Hebrew, it's *be-lev va-lev*—they speak "with a heart and with a heart." They have two hearts in them!

VAN DOREN:   I've never forgotten that won-   PSALM
derful line, "The Lord is nigh unto them that are of   34: 19
a broken heart."

SAMUEL:   Yes, and "a broken and a contrite   PSALM
heart." Or the Psalmist says, "The fool hath said in his   51: 19
heart: 'There is no God.' "   PSALM
14: 1

VAN DOREN:   By the way, Maurice, what is
the Hebrew word which is translated "heart"? Is it the
same thing that we understand it to be?

SAMUEL:   *Lev*—literally, the heart itself.

VAN DOREN:   The same organ?

SAMUEL:   It is the organ within the body, and
it is a very wonderful word because it is put into doz-
ens of forms. For example, you remember that wonderful phrase, "Thou hast ravished my heart." It's one   SONG 4:9
word in Hebrew, *libavtini,* based on *lev,* heart; and it
means, "You have taken my heart captive," or "filled
my heart," or "given me a new heart." Or there's a
phrase which has gone into the daily prayers of the
synagogue: "Let the words of my mouth and the medi-   PSALM
tation of my heart be acceptable before Thee." And by   19: 15
the way, for the parallel to the heart, we have: "Test
my reins and my heart."[8] There's another interesting   PSALM 26:2
use of that word: "He that fashioneth the hearts of   PSALM
[men] . . . ." That is to say, the ancients had, one might   33: 15

almost say, a modern psychological approach, in that
they indicated the depth of an emotion by the response
which it actually provoked in the physical being of the
man.

VAN DOREN:   By the way, Maurice, a moment ago you spoke of Pascal, who was certainly one
of the great psychologists of religion. I think he was
a very great man. You remember his famous statement
about the mind and the heart. That was not a sentimen-
tal statement for him at all.

SAMUEL:   He said in his *Pensées,* "The heart
has its reasons which reason does not know." It's put
very charmingly by a modern and very much neglected poet, Ralph Hodgson, who says:

> *Reason has moons, but moons not hers*
> *Lie mirrored on her sea,*
> *Confounding her astronomers,*
> *But O! delighting me.*[9]

VAN DOREN *(laughing):*   Very fine!

SAMUEL:   The Psalmist's compulsive preoccupation with the physical structure of the world as one
of the means—I'd say the *supreme* means—of expressing for the ordinary man the attitude toward God *is*
what makes the Bible in general, and the Book of
Psalms in particular, the intellectual book without intellectuality.

VAN DOREN:   That's exactly what I was trying
to say! There's no doubt that a beautiful intellect is

operating throughout, but it is operating in the way
that the intellect of poetry operates: it is searching for
evidences, watching for every movement, every
sound; it is listening for testimonies that the whole
world somehow is uttering. The physical world of the
Psalmist is very active, and very vocal: the mountains          PSALM
"skip like rams"—you can actually *see* the mountains          114:6
skipping! And of course, there are winds. That word
"winds" is a very powerful word, wouldn't you say?

SAMUEL: Yes, it has a double force. The
word *ruach* in Hebrew means both "wind" and a
"spirit."[10] It can be an indwelling spirit, and it can be
the physical wind, the winds of Aeolus, if you like, the
pagan wind, as it were.

VAN DOREN: If I may, I'd like to go on
enumerating some of those images which will recur in
our discussions. There are trees, of course, too: the          *e.g.* PSALM
palm tree and the cedars of Lebanon—trees are of the           92:13
utmost importance here. He who meditates in His law            PSALM
day and night "shall be like a tree planted by streams         1:2–3
of water, That bringeth forth its fruit in its season, And
whose leaf doth not wither"—vigorous, healthy,
beautiful trees are the very image of spiritual health
here. And not only trees, but water—water in every
form, the seas, streams, still waters . . . .

SAMUEL: "He leadeth me beside the still wa-          PSALM 23:2
ters."

VAN DOREN: And the deeps. There's a great          PSALM 36:7
line: "Thy judgments are like the great deep."

PSALM
69:3,2
SAMUEL:    And floods, as well as waters: "the flood overwhelmeth me"; and *bah-u mayim ad nah-fesh,"* the waters are come in even unto the soul." The Psalmist is always using the physical, the plastic, the "feelable." He talks about things that you handle, or touch; and in the "handling" of these, there flows into you the feeling of gratitude, appreciation, or whatever you want to call it, of the created world—the created world as itself being a poem, an utterance.

VAN DOREN:    It's as if God had made the world almost as a musical instrument upon which we can play. Here are the trees, and here are the winds, and here are the seas and the streams; here is water, here is dry land, and here, of course, are the animals —the creatures other than ourselves—whom we can constantly bring into our speech, playing upon them very much as a great musician might play upon a many-stringed lyre.

*see* PSALM
148
SAMUEL:    You get that feeling especially in the great lyrical outburst at the end of the Book of Psalms, where *everything* praises God—creeping things, the mountains, the blades of grass, everything that is in the world is a praise of God. In the conception of the Psalmist, the world is a psalm; the commentators dwell with a great deal of insistence on this. Even the dead things, as we see them, are interpenetrated. It's interesting, Mark, that the modern philosopher sometimes talks of matter as being "psychoidal," that is to say, that there couldn't have emerged a thing like "mind" or "psyche" from dead matter if dead matter itself didn't have within itself implicitly the

possibility of a psyche. This is what the Psalmist has seen without any of the devices of the modern psychologist, just as he saw—anticipated, really—what the modern scientist has often said: "God is a mathematician." That is putting it, in my opinion, a little bit too baldly; it's like the critic's view of Kipling, who accused the poet of describing God as though He were a Scots engineer steering a boat! God as a "mathematician"—yes, if you see that aspect as occupying its proper place within the setting of all the other attributes of God. The writers of the Bible anticipated that when they talked of God making the world and meting out waters "by measure." But certainly, He made JOB 28:25 it not merely "by measure," and this is only one of the innumerable forms of appreciation of the diversity and colorfulness of the world.

VAN DOREN:   Maurice, I would make the same protest against anyone who said that God was a poet. He made a world which poets can use to praise Him or to express Him.

SAMUEL:   I agree with you, Mark. Poets are great things, but they aren't that good!

VAN DOREN:   No!

SAMUEL:   I mean, they aren't quite the equivalent of God!

VAN DOREN:   No! Poetry is not that important, neither is mathematics. But both are very, very important modes of understanding. That brings me

back to a few more of these recurrent images, Maurice. Think of the parts of the body in the psalms, in addition to the heart: the tongue, the lips, the teeth, *see* PSALM the bones. "The crushed bones"—in one of the psalms
51:10 of despair, the Psalmist speaks as if he had been literally torn apart.

PSALM SAMUEL: "I am poured out like water, And
22:15 all my bones are out of joint; . . ."

VAN DOREN: And the lips which conceal the
*see* PSALM tongue of the serpent and the venom of vipers. Of
140:4 course, to go back to more physical things, there's
PSALM
103:15 grass: man's "days are as grass."

PSALM 90:6 SAMUEL: Yes, "In the morning it flourisheth, and groweth up; In the evening it is cut down, and withereth." You know, Mark, what you've just said is particularly interesting because you reconstituted this image of man as being a kind of cosmos—man as the whole world—and that is the way the Jewish mystics, particularly in the Kabbalah,[11] have seen man. They have taken him, the human being, and turned him into an image of the cosmos. This gets its lead from what you've just observed, that in the psalms particularly, every part of the human being has a religious function, and it is to be used in the attempt at the lyrical appraisal of God's relationship to man.

VAN DOREN: I think you're referring to something that used to be called the "microcosm."

SAMUEL: That's right, yes!

VAN DOREN: Man is the cosmos in little; everything in the cosmos is condensed in him somehow, and it's in him, ticketed; and each part of him can be separated out and made to refer to something.

SAMUEL: Let me interrupt, Mark. James Joyce tried to do that also in his *Ulysses*. In the wanderings of his hero through the city of Dublin, he tried to project the image of the wanderings of Odysseus. In various sections, he used the parts of the body almost in a kabbalistic attempt to recreate a cosmos in the man himself.[12] I'm sorry, you were going to say . . .

VAN DOREN: No, I'm glad you interrupted to mention that. Joyce tried to do more of the same thing in his very last book, *Finnegans Wake*—he did more of it more elaborately and almost bafflingly.

SAMUEL: Too elaborately for me, by the way.

VAN DOREN: For me, too.

SAMUEL: I've never struggled through that last book.

VAN DOREN: Returning to these images, there's not only water in great variety and great quantity as a most lovely thing in the Book of Psalms, but there are other liquids, too—honey, oil. You remember: "Behold, how good and how pleasant it is/ For brethren to dwell together in unity!/ It is like the precious oil upon the head,/ Coming down upon the beard; . . ." PSALM 133:1-2

SAMUEL:   Is this a poetic hyperbole, do you think, or did they literally *pour* it on? Yes, they would anoint a man's head with oil, and even that, I suppose, was a symbolic gesture. But does it mean that they poured it on, until it ran over his beard and his moustache? Was it supposed to be *enjoyed?* That's one of the things that's baffled me, and I don't know how literally it ought to be taken.

*(laughter)*

VAN DOREN:   No, it does sound excessive, although very charming! Of course, there's "night," too, as well as "day." The Psalmist is often lying upon his bed meditating, as he puts it in one place: ". . . I remember Thee upon my couch,/ And meditate on Thee in the night-watches." "Night-watches" is a term that comes in often, too. These are the great fundamental images, by the way, in all poetry: night, day, animals. The animals that are here I shall want to talk about later, but I suppose the commonest symbol of the vicious or dangerous animal is the lion.

PSALM 63:7

SAMUEL:   The lion keeps on recurring in the psalms. What's interesting, though, is that several Hebrew words are used for that: *aryeh* is lion, and *kephir* is a young lion.

VAN DOREN:   I didn't know that!

SAMUEL:   It strikes you with an additional force in the Hebrew—as though when the lion has

grown from a certain stage to the majesty of comple-
tion, it has taken on a new personality.

VAN DOREN:    The lion who walks the streets
is familiar to us from the Book of Proverbs, but we      *see*
find him in the psalms too, preying upon the lamb. Of    PROVERBS
course, he's the violent man, the vicious man, who       22:13;
victimizes the poor, the needy, and the orphan. The      26:13
poor and the needy are ever present in the psalms, too,  *e.g.,*
wouldn't you say?                                        PSALMS
                                                         9:19; 12:6;
                                                         72:12

SAMUEL:    Oh, yes! But there's so much to say,
I'm a bit perplexed.

VAN DOREN:    There's just one more, and
then I'll stop. I hope I haven't pursued this matter too
far.

SAMUEL:    You can't! Each of them is very
tempting, and can be used with a great deal of il-
luminative effect.

VAN DOREN:    There's the "pit." When we
once discussed the Joseph story,[13] we talked about the
immense significance of the pit into which Joseph was
thrown, the pit into which the soul descended. The
image could be used in all sorts of ways. Egypt, for
example, was a pit into which the whole people descended, deprived as they were of their own native
land. But the pit here often appears as something that   *e.g.,* PSALM
has been dug for our hurt; but the digger of the pit      7:16
falls into it himself.

SAMUEL:  Yes! There's always that note: if a man digs a pit, he's going to fall into it himself, and it is the symbol of the wicked man overreaching himself. Wickedness is something which, in the end, is bound to lead to self-destruction. We're going to talk more of this particular image when we come to examine the aspect under which wickedness is presented in the psalms. But while we're on this subject of the use of the sensuous, the "feelable," for the illumination of the intellectual (I must use that word!), the body as the instrument of expression of the mind, I can't help adverting to the tremendous concern which the Psalmist shows with truthfulness to oneself. He pleads with God, "Create me a clean heart." When he speaks of proud people as "Their heart is gross like fat"—the heart got fatted up!—he seems to be continuously aware of the power of self-deception in human beings. What he means by a "clean heart" is—I'm going to use the modern terminology—"Prevent me from rationalizing"; that is to say, "Don't let me mislead myself by giving a false reason and thus covering up some misdemeanor, or claiming a credit to which I'm not entitled." By the way, now that I've mentioned the word, it is one of the oddities of modern terminology that the word "rationalized" is used in an absolutely inverse sense. When we "rationalize" an industry, we put some common sense into it. But when we're "rationalizing" a wish, we're doing the very opposite: we're committing a stupidity! We're being irrational when we rationalize.

PSALM 51:12
PSALM 119:70

VAN DOREN *(laughing)*:  Exactly! We're fooling ourselves. And of course, one of the commonest forms of this is found in the man who confesses to some kind of shortcoming in himself, with the full expectation that you will say, "But ah, that is after all a virtue!" or "It's the defect of a virtue!"

SAMUEL: Yes, he expects you always to say, "Now, *you're* the kind of man I like!"

VAN DOREN: Yes, "You have this weakness."

SAMUEL: Now this is the thing that the Psalmist girds at, and he is tremendously troubled by it. Do you know, there's another way of putting it: some years ago, an English newspaper ran a competition, in which a series of parallels of three were given. For instance: "I am firm. You are obstinate. That fellow is pig-headed." All three meant the same thing— and this is the danger of rationalization!

# III

# DAVID,
# THE GREAT PSALMODIST

.

SAMUEL: Mark, I'm afraid that we have to give up what has been fascinating us a great deal in the last two talks—namely, the general examination of the power and the beauty of the Book of Psalms—and move on to specific analyses of the material we have in our minds. I'm sure that the material you have in *your* mind is enough to fill all these conversations.

VAN DOREN: Yes, I could talk about it forever, I think.

SAMUEL: Yes! Well, we've got to get down to some of the specific aspects. I suppose we can't do that without first discussing the central figure of David as the great Psalmodist—not that all the psalms were written by him, or are even attributed to him.

VAN DOREN: Some of them could not have been written by him, since they refer to events centuries after he died—the great 137th Psalm, for example, which refers to the Babylonian exile.[14]

SAMUEL: Some of the psalms are attributed to others—Psalm 90, for instance, is actually attributed to Moses. It starts out, "A Prayer of Moses the man of God." The Book of Psalms contains one hundred fifty psalms; of these, seventy-three carry the heading, *Mizmor le'David,* or simply, *Le'David.*[15] That might mean "David's Hymn of Praise," or "A Song of David"; but the commentators note that others could have written them, and thus the Hebrew heading might be translated also as "Psalm *in the style of* David," or a "Davidic hymn," or "concerning" or "for David." However, David, who is called in the Bible "the sweet singer of Israel," has forever been known as *the* Psalmist; other psalmodists may or may not have fashioned themselves on him, but he set the pattern. A second feature of the psalms that makes people associate the name "David" with them is the explanatory information which appears at the beginning of some of them—for example, Psalm 3 opens: "A Psalm of David, when he fled from Absalom his son"; and Psalm 51, "A Psalm of David when Nathan the prophet came unto him after he had gone in to Bathsheba," which appears to be a reference to the famous episode in the Book of Samuel.

II SAM. 23:1

II SAM. 11–12

VAN DOREN:   One illustration that occurs to me is Psalm 72, the one David presumably sang at the moment when he knew that his son, Solomon, was to succeed him as king.

SAMUEL:   Yes, that's one of the great moralistic psalms. It's what we would call in Hebrew David's *tsava'ah,* his ethical will, giving his instructions to Solomon on the proper duties of the king. We'll come back to discuss Psalm 72 in detail, but first, I thought it would be well just to run very rapidly through the career of David, in order to provide a setting for the references to various situations and incidents in his life. You remember that the Lord was disappointed in Saul's performance as king and He sent the prophet Samuel to anoint David, the youngest son of Jesse, as the successor to the throne. The young David goes from Bethlehem to the king's court, where he becomes Saul's armor-bearer. David evidently has great ability in playing the harp, and his music soothes the king. At about this time, David volunteers to face Goliath, and he kills the giant. David and Jonathan, the king's son, form a great friendship. David fights the battles of Saul, and soon his relationship with the king is disrupted. Saul conceives a hostility toward David—a hostility based in fear. David runs away from Saul, who is ready to murder him. The king and his men pursue David up and down the land. David becomes an outlaw, the head of a band of rebels.

I SAM.
16–17

VAN DOREN:   By the way, David has opportunities to kill Saul. He refuses to injure him.

SAMUEL: Yes! It occurs to me: it's very strange that throughout the psalms, you find David complaining about Saul, and very often using him, it would seem, as the prototype of a wicked man, a persecutor. Yet in the historical narrative itself, David always treats Saul with respect. On two occasions, you remember, he could have taken the life of Saul, but he didn't. He calls him, "my father," and he refers to himself as "a single flea." He never speaks disrespectfully, let alone resentfully, of Saul. I'm very often puzzled by those headings in the psalms, and I wonder if there was so much reference originally to the personal situation between the two. What we have to bear in mind in David's career is that there *was* this terrible struggle between him and the king; that he *did* come to replace King Saul; and that there were occasions when he could have felt a deep unhappiness, even a certain amount of bitterness. But I can't straighten out in my mind the contradiction between David's reverential attitude in the narrative portion, where he refers to Saul as "the Lord's anointed," and his bitter outpouring in the Book of Psalms, where on at least one occasion he compares his enemy to a ravening lion.

I SAM. 24:12; 26:20

*see* PSALM 17:12

VAN DOREN: It's one of the most interesting relationships between two men that I know—the relations between Saul and David, don't you think so?

SAMUEL: Yes, and at the end, when the young man comes and boasts that he killed Saul, David is taken aback in horror, and says, "You dared to lift your hand against the anointed of God?" He has the man slain! Then again, I'm very much astonished that

*see* II SAM. 1:14-15

there isn't a single psalm in which David celebrates his famous friendship with Jonathan. There are words of praise, and of regretful remembering on the part of David with regard to Saul—but no expression of joy and love with regard to Saul's son.

VAN DOREN:   David could be said, perhaps, to have loved Saul partly because Saul was Jonathan's father. They were a pair for him, and he laments them both.

SAMUEL:   Yes, but you could call that lament —that famous lament at the beginning of Second Samuel—a psalm.

*see* II SAM.
I:19–27

VAN DOREN:   Yes, and one of the greatest!

SAMUEL:   It's a psalm of lament: "How are the mighty fallen,/ And the weapons of war perished!" And it goes on: "Saul and Jonathan, the lovely and the pleasant/ In their lives, even in their death they were not divided . . ." Now this lament is very specifically identified; but generally speaking, the contradictions and the omissions I've just cited make me hesitant about accepting at their face value these attributions of psalms to particular situations—although I must say, they very often fit, don't they?

VAN DOREN:   Yes. Now for instance, there's the 51st Psalm that you mentioned. The conventional interpretation sees that as David's song of repentance for his sin in having Uriah the Hittite murdered, and in taking Uriah's wife, Bathsheba, to become his queen. To be sure, neither of these persons is mentioned in Psalm 51, yet it's almost unmistakable, don't you think?

SAMUEL:   It begs itself to be associated! The psalm mirrors the mood of David depicted in the narrative of the historical book: we see the breakdown of the man's ego. He was shattered by the death of the child, and he took that devastating rebuke administered by the prophet Nathan. That rebuke, by the way, is one of the most remarkable episodes in the history of man, I would say. Here is a court prophet telling an absolute king, "Thou art the man." And King David never says a word! This contrition David shows does beg itself to be transferred to the most contrite psalm of all—Psalm 51.

II SAM.
12: 7

VAN DOREN:   The wisdom of calling the book "The Psalms of David" seems to me proved by two facts: David's own character and his ability to feel. His character is one of the richest and deepest of all among the men of the Bible. He was a passionate man, a man who erred greatly, as well as a man who knew everything about righteousness. He was a man who sinned, and who did not sin—both magnificently. He was a man who felt everything that happened to him more deeply than any other man. David's capacity to feel is bottomless, and a very beautiful thing. That qualifies him, it seems to me, to be the author of these poems, and I'm perfectly willing to go on calling them "The Psalms of David."

SAMUEL:   Yes, he set the style.

VAN DOREN:    And furthermore, there is the
fact that David is always referred to as a poet and a
musician, even a dancer.

SAMUEL:    He danced before the Ark of the
*see* II SAM.   Lord, to the dismay and derision of his wife, Michal.
6:16

VAN DOREN:    He was an artist—a skillful artist, knowing all the techniques of an art. As I say, I
should be perfectly willing and content to go on thinking of David as *the* Psalmist, even though there are
psalms which he could not have written.

SAMUEL:    And to which his name is not attached. A dozen of the psalms—Psalm 50 and Psalms
73 to 83—are attributed to a man named Asaph, a
musician and David's contemporary.[16] Some of the
psalms have no heading at all. There's another reason
that supports your attitude on this, Mark: diffused
through the psalms is a constant reference to the shepherd's craft and the shepherd's care. (You remember
how that was mirrored again in Milton's *Lycidas.*)
Over and over again, we have references to the shep-
PSALM        herd and his flock: "Thou hast given us like sheep to
44:12        be eaten . . ."; "We are accounted as sheep for the
44:23
49:15        slaughter . . ."; "Like sheep they are appointed for the
nether-world; Death shall be their shepherd"; and
there's the very beautiful image which everybody
PSALM 23:1    knows, "The Lord is my shepherd, . . ."

VAN DOREN:    Maurice, we were speaking of
David's relationship with Saul. Psalm 57, which is described as "A Psalm of David, when he fled from Saul,

in the cave," perhaps might be an expression of his   I SAM. 24
feelings during that episode at En-gedi, but the reference could be to any kind of enemies:

> *My soul is among lions, I do lie down among them that are*   PSALM
>   *aflame;*   57:5–12
> *Even the sons of men, whose teeth are spears and arrows,*
> *And their tongue a sharp sword.*
> *Be Thou exalted, O God, above the heavens;*
> *Thy glory be above all the earth.*

I want to emphasize the word "above" because later
on, that will be emphasized again.

> *They have prepared a net for my steps,*
> *My soul is bowed down;*
> *They have digged a pit before me,*
> *They have fallen into the midst thereof themselves.*
> *My heart is stedfast, O God, my heart is stedfast;*
> *I will sing, yea, I will sing praises.*
> *Awake, my glory; awake, psaltery and harp;*
> *I will awake the dawn.*
> *I will give thanks unto Thee, O Lord, among the peoples;*
> *I will sing praises unto Thee among the nations.*
> *For Thy mercy is great unto the heavens,*
> *And Thy truth unto the skies.*
> *Be Thou exalted, O God, above the heavens;*
> *Thy glory be above all the earth.*

That word "above," it seems to me, is of tremendous
significance there. Notice he says: "Thy mercy is great
*unto* the heavens," as if it could reach that far; and
"Thy truth" is great enough to reach *as far as* the skies.
And then suddenly he says: "But it's *above* them, too."
It's greater and more inclusive.

SAMUEL:   You mentioned that you could take

this as referring to David fleeing from Saul, or to a man fleeing from the adversary generally. What is characteristic of the psalms—of those attributed directly to David, and those not attributed to him at all —is that the individual very often changes places with the community, and you can't tell whether it is a man who is offering up a prayer, or whether it is a communal prayer. This is characteristic of Jewish worship generally, by the way, in which the individual as a rule is certainly not eclipsed, but made to mingle with the congregation. That is, the congregation carries him, and he carries the congregation. This runs through the psalms, and the psalms have become the stay of Jewish prayer—in the daily prayers, in the Sabbath prayers, and in the prayers of the High Holy Days. The psalms keep recurring again and again.

VAN DOREN:   I suppose, Maurice, you do not have religion unless there is this possibility of identification, even confusion, between the individual and the whole people. Everything is true for each person; but also, everything is true for all. They *all* understand and believe the same things. Wasn't that what you were saying?

SAMUEL:   Yes, but there can be an important difference of emphasis, that is to say, whether a man thinks of his personal salvation as being the primary consideration, or whether he thinks of the community as being *the* important consideration. It's a matter of emphasis, and not of exclusivity, and this emphasis can be important. In the case of the Jews, I would say that the emphasis rests definitely upon the people. For example, the question of individual immortality for the Jew is practically absent from the *Tanach,* the Hebrew Bible. There are, of course, arguments that these-and-these verses refer to the subject, and they can be given such an interpretation. But the individual Jew plays a smaller role than elsewhere; it is the immortality of the *community* which is the concern of the individual Jew and of the congregation.

VAN DOREN:   And of course, an individual himself, speaking or singing here in the psalms, from time to time says, "I will praise the Lord while I live." It's "while I live," because "The dead praise not the Lord." In other words, "How can I praise Thee when I'm dead?"

PSALM
146:2

115:17

SAMUEL:   There's a very striking abhorrence of death in the Book of Psalms—a feeling that death is the end of everything, and of "What use will I be to You when I am dead?" In my opinion—I don't know how you feel about it—that attitude would be consonant with a man like David who lived himself out tremendously. He was a great liver. He loved, he hated, he fought, he suffered, he sinned, he repented —with a prodigality of emotion and of motion.

VAN DOREN:   And he grieved as no other man could grieve.

SAMUEL:   Yes! The servants were afraid to go to tell him that his child by Bathsheba was dead. He saw them whispering together, and in effect said to them what Hamlet said of Rosencrantz and Guilden-

*see* II SAM.
12:18

stern, "I have an eye of you!—I know what you're up to!" The child was dead and they were afraid to tell him!

VAN DOREN:    And there is also that marvelous moment when David had grieved so long over Absalom that Joab, his general, went to him and said: *see* II SAM. 19:6 "Listen, if you keep on grieving like this, it will appear to the people that you are sorry that our enemy has been defeated." And nothing is more eloquent in the whole Bible, it seems to me, than the response of David: he simply gets up and walks away! He stops grieving. He doesn't say, "I shall stop." He just *does!*

SAMUEL:    He does that also, you remember, in the case of the child. He had fasted, he had prayed, he had prostrated himself before God that the child should live, but God had decreed that it should die. And his servants were terrified to tell him of the death. When the child was dead, he got up, washed, anointed himself, and changed his garments, and went and ate. He said very calmly, "While the child lived, there was hope. But now"—these are terribly moving words, and they belong so thoroughly to David!—"[the II SAM. 12:23 child] is dead, wherefore should I fast? can I bring him back again? I shall go to him, but he will not return to me." There is something heartbreaking in the simplicity of that statement: "It's finished. It's over!" And it's consonant again with the character of David throughout the psalms—that death finishes all.

Let me go on a little with David as the setting for the psalms. I want to correlate the David that is given to us in the Book of Psalms with the David in the historical books. You've noticed, of course, that one of the psalms, Psalm 18, is actually taken from— or has been put into—the historical book of Second Samuel 22. This psalm is very interesting because it is surrounded by the material of David's life. What you get in the Book of Psalms is the distillation. Sometimes I've wondered: How did David write the psalms? Was it much later, when he thought back upon a given situation? Or was it almost, say, the same night, after a battle? Would he reach for his harp restlessly just after the incident was over? But in any case, we have some of the background of David's adventures:

> *And the Philistines had war again with Israel; and David went down, and his servants with him, and fought against the Philistines; and David waxed faint. And Ishbi-benob, who was of the sons of the giant, the weight of whose spear was three hundred shekels of brass in weight, he being girded with new armour, thought to have slain David. But Abishai the son of Zeruiah succoured him, and smote the Philistine, and killed him. Then the men of David swore unto him, saying: "Thou shalt go no more out with us to battle, that thou quench not the lamp of Israel."*

II SAM.
21:15ff.

They knew what David was. He was not just a king. But he *did* go on, because immediately after that, this is what happens:

> *And it came to pass after this, that there was again war with the Philistines at Gob; then Sibbecai the Hushathite slew Saph, who was of the sons of the giant.*

You know, the Philistines seem to abound in giants!

VAN DOREN *(laughing)*:   Yes!

SAMUEL:   They're an extraordinary race!

*And there was again war with the Philistines at Gob; and Elhanan the son of Jaare-oregim the Beth-lehemite slew Goliath the Gittite, . . .*

Curious, by the way—another Goliath than the one who was killed by David, or a repetition of the story.

*. . . the staff of whose spear was like a weaver's beam. And there was again war at Gath, where was a champion, that had on every hand six fingers, and on every foot six toes, four and twenty in number; and he also was born to the giant. And when he taunted Israel, Jonathan the son of Shimea David's brother slew him.*

These are tremendous events. The man is a fighter, but you get a setting. For example, the tenderness of the men toward him, saying, "Don't go forth to battle anymore," gives us the view of his own contemporaries toward him. David, not heeding their admonition, goes out to fight nevertheless; and we're told about a certain interesting incident:

II SAM.
23:13–17
*And three of the thirty chief went down, and came to David in the harvest time unto the cave of Adullam; and the troop of the Philistines were encamped in the valley of Rephaim. And David was then in the stronghold, and the garrison of the Philistines was then in Beth-lehem. And David longed, and said: "Oh that one would give me water to drink of the well of Bethlehem, which is by the gate!" And the three mighty men broke through the host of the Philistines, and drew water out of the well of Beth-lehem, that was by the gate, and took it, and brought it to David; but he would not drink thereof,*

*but poured it out unto the Lord. And he said: "Be it far from me, O Lord, that I should do this; shall I drink the blood of the men that went in jeopardy of their lives?" therefore he would not drink it. These things did the three mighty men.*

Now there is David the Psalmist! When people wonder how this man could have been the fighter and the singer, the warrior and the poet—well, you see here a composite character. All of this is in great consonance with the observation you made: this is the man to whom the Book of Psalms as a whole should be attributed, irrespective of the individual psalms.

VAN DOREN:   Yes, those fascinating passages you've just cited reveal another dimension of David, in addition to those we mentioned earlier. He was a great warrior, of course—a warrior who even in the midst of battle, nevertheless could do some very simple thing and strike his opponents. He was an extraordinary person!

SAMUEL:   This incident of the water reminds one a little of that famous story of Sir Philip Sidney dying at the Battle of Zutphen,[17] doesn't it?—giving the water to another soldier whose need was greater. But if we're going to speak of David's authorship literally, we can always cite the last verse of Psalm 72, which perhaps was added later:

*The prayers of David the son of Jesse are ended.*          PSALM 72:20

Also, again in Second Samuel, we have:

II SAM.  *Now these are the last words of David:*
23:1–3  *The saying of David the son of Jesse,*
*And the saying of the man raised on high,*
*The anointed of the God of Jacob,*
*And the sweet singer of Israel:*
*The spirit of the Lord spoke by me,*
*And His word was upon my tongue.*

*The God of Israel said,*
*The Rock of Israel spoke to me: . . .*

That is given as the last psalm of David. We don't have
to take this literally. We don't have to take the
chronology of the events as being precisely as they are
put there. What is of importance is to realize that the
interplay between the character of the Book of Psalms
and the character of King David gives a certain
warmth, a certain human fullness to the psalms, even
when we take them as being the production of many,
many centuries, and of many, many varieties of men.

VAN DOREN:   And of course, there's still a
further dimension of David that is indicated in Psalm
110. There he is a priest:

PSALM   *The Lord hath sworn, and will not repent:*
110:4   *"Thou art a priest for ever*
*After the manner of Melchizedek."*

That fascinates me! Melchizedek, the priest and king
of Salem, appears just for a second of time in the Book
of Genesis, in order to bless Abraham and to bring
GEN. 14:18   him bread and wine. He's never mentioned before or
after that one reference, is he?

SAMUEL:   No, but he's made much of in the

Jewish legends, which say that he might have been the founder of the Jewish religion if it hadn't been for some minor misdemeanor of his which put a blemish on him.[18]

VAN DOREN:   Yes, but this suggests that David is not only a priestly person as well as a warrior, a lover, a sinner, and a singer, but that he is of the prime order of priests. He's a great original priest-king like Melchizedek.

# IV

## FROM THE PERSONAL
## TO THE UNIVERSAL

SAMUEL: Mark, we were talking last time about David's peculiar association with the Book of Psalms. He occupies two positions—one, as the author of the psalms, or at least as the hero of the psalmodic mode in ancient Jewish writing; and the other, as a historical figure. We noted some of the contrasts and congruences between the two roles, finding some of the psalms suited with peculiar appositeness to the historical circumstances; and we also observed the spread from the personal—that is, applying to David himself—to universal needs. For instance, you mentioned the very famous and—well, "popular" would be an incongruous word—one of the most loved of all the psalms—Psalm 51.

VAN DOREN: Yes, there's a great beauty in Psalm 51. It goes very deep into human suffering after sin:

> *Be gracious unto me, O God, according to Thy mercy;*     PSALM
> *According to the multitude of Thy compassions blot out my*  51:3–10
>    *transgressions.*
> *Wash me thoroughly from mine iniquity,*
> *And cleanse me from my sin.*
> *For I know my transgressions;*
> *And my sin is ever before me. . . .*
> *Behold, I was brought forth in iniquity,*
> *And in sin did my mother conceive me.* [19]
> *Behold, Thou desirest truth in the inward parts;*
> *Make me, therefore, to know wisdom in mine inmost heart.*
> *Purge me with hyssop, and I shall be clean;*
> *Wash me, and I shall be whiter than snow.*
> *Make me to hear joy and gladness;*
> *That the bones which Thou hast crushed may rejoice.*

SAMUEL: There's a very great power there: a man in almost absolute despair as to his inner constitution, and the only hope he has is that God will help him to get rid of these—as we would say in modern language—"complexes," these inwoven evil impulses of his.

VAN DOREN: Of course, for me it's very characteristic of David to say: "I know my transgressions. My sin is ever before me." He was not the kind of man to dodge or hedge at such a point. Once Nathan the Prophet had persuaded him of his sin, notified him of it, as it were—because it might mean that he hadn't somehow been aware before of it—the knowledge of it suddenly possessed him, and there was no "rationalization" on his part at all, to use the word you brought up earlier. The frankness, the simplicity with which David conceded sin is to me one of the most moving and admirable things about him.

SAMUEL:   You know, there is today very popular in psychology the phrase, "guilt complex" People, we say, have "a guilt complex," and it's generally taken to be a condition of which a person must rid himself, *not* by recognizing that he *is* guilty (because that's the guilt complex); instead, he is supposed to get rid of any oppression as to having been a wrongdoer. I think this is the very opposite of the moral intention of the Bible as a whole, as pointed up particularly in this psalm. He *knows* what he did, and he *was* guilty. It wasn't a guilt complex, it was a genuine guilt.

VAN DOREN:   That's right. And he recognizes so frankly and completely that he has been shattered by the knowledge: "the bones which Thou hast crushed"—we spoke of that image in our second talk. It's an extreme, all but excessive, image—and yet it isn't excessive, either, because he convinces you that it's right. I remember suddenly a line out of Shakespeare's *Othello.* Othello says, "My heart is turned to stone." He makes a gesture of striking his breast, and he says, "I strike it, and it hurts my hand." There's a metaphor that becomes literalized: his heart is really a sharp stone, it hurts him to strike it. So here, the bones of David have been crushed; he has been shattered by this, and to be sure, he's ready to be made over again.

SAMUEL:   Yes, that is what the verse says. You
lead up to it that way. Toward the end of the psalm,
David says:

> For Thou delightest not in sacrifice, else would I give it;
> Thou hast no pleasure in burnt-offering.
> The sacrifices of God are a broken spirit;
> A broken and a contrite heart, O God, Thou wilt not despise.

PSALM
51:18–19

This again, I find to be in contradiction to most of the
tendencies of modern psychologists whose aim it is to
"build a man up"; to make one feel, "No, I wasn't
guilty. I had a complex; there were circumstances
which led me to it." But David says very specifically,
"The sacrifices of God are a broken spirit." To *know*
that you have been wicked, and to be shattered by it!
Then notice, Mark, the thing we referred to tangentially last time, and here it is again: it isn't just one
person who's talking (although it is intensely a man
who's talking), but it is the voice of the people also.
The people of Israel and David become fused. After
acknowledging that God wants a broken spirit and a
contrite heart, David goes on to say:

> Do good in Thy favour unto Zion;
> Build Thou the walls of Jerusalem.
> Then wilt Thou delight in the sacrifices of righteousness, in
>     burnt-offering and whole offering;
> Then will they offer bullocks upon Thine altar.

PSALM
51:20–21

In other words, this man speaks for himself, and by
the *intensity* of his concentration on his own problems, becomes an utterance for his people, and—as
it has turned out—for the whole of the Western
world.

VAN DOREN:   Yes, of course. That is his final importance. He is not only the supreme individual that we know, but as the typical poet in the psalms, he is the spokesman of a people. I might ask you, Maurice, if you can help me to understand in any special way verse 16 of Psalm 51: "Deliver me from bloodguiltiness." David had been the cause of the death of Uriah the Hittite, and I suddenly remember a moment earlier in his life when he and his young men started out on an expedition to put to death Nabal the farmer. Nabal, who is described as "churlish" by his own wife, Abigail,[20] had stupidly refused to give tribute to David's men. Abigail, hearing that this expedition was forward, rushed out to meet David and his forces with presents and asses loaded with delicious food. On seeing David, she dismounted, knelt before him, and warned him that if he proceeded to execute his purpose, he would be guilty of shedding blood. That seems to have moved him, because David then blessed her: ". . . thou . . . hast kept me this day from bloodguiltiness." But in what sense in Psalm 51 could he ask God to deliver him from bloodguiltiness without any trial among men, or anything of the sort?

*see* I SAM. 25

I SAM. 25:33

SAMUEL:   As the king, David had already arranged for the death of Uriah. David didn't commit the murder by his own hand, but he had ordered it. I think he means in that verse 16: "Deliver me from the impulse to shed blood."

VAN DOREN:   I see—shed blood *henceforth.*

SAMUEL:   Yes, in the future. The sin of the past can be wiped out only by the fact that you don't commit that sin again in the future. When a man says, "I repent," and then goes on to repeat the sin, then he has not repented. In saying, "Deliver me from blood-guiltiness," he means, "Make my past clean by the fact that my future will be clean." The reference might be specifically to his murder of Uriah the Hittite, and it might be to his career as a whole. You remember that in the historical narrative, David tells Solomon that he had wanted to build the Temple, but the Lord told him that he had shed so much blood that it would be for Solomon to build the house of the Lord. The blood might have been that of the enemies of Israel, and it might have been the blood of his personal enemies; and for that reason, the supreme achievment of erecting the Temple of God, which was to serve all nations, was withheld from David.

*see* I CHRON. 22:8

VAN DOREN: As you were saying last time, Maurice, he was punished immediately for the death of Uriah by the death of his child by Bathsheba.

SAMUEL: And he grieved over it in such a way as to make the entourage fear for his reason. If I may, Mark, let me pause a little over this curious phenomenon of David—David, the eponym of his people, David the representative of the people who merges with the people, and David the individual. How little there is in the Book of Psalms of reference to David's own specific circumstances! There's no mention of his family, and in particular, there's no mention of his mother anywhere in the Bible, let alone in the psalms. The *midrashim,* the collection of Jewish legends and commentaries which have grown up over thousands of years, are fairly copious about David's father.

VAN DOREN: You mean Jesse?

SAMUEL: Jesse, the father of David. He was supposed to be a great scholar. There are quaint stories about him: how he was in love with one of his slaves, and how David's mother (called Nazbat in legend) substituted herself for that slave, and that was how David was begotten. Therefore, according to the legends,[21] David as a child bore the stigma of being the offspring of a slave. They tried to build up what wasn't given in the narrative, because David did so sink into the consciousness of the people as representing the people that, as a person within the psalms, he disappears; whereas he is very much of a person in the narrative books.

VAN DOREN: Yes, in the narratives we read a wealth of details about his principal wives and children. No one ever forgets that one of his sons was Absalom, for instance, and another was Amnon. We know the names of his chief wives, and how he came to marry them. And above all, we know about Solomon. In this connection, Psalm 72 interests me. Although Solomon's name is not mentioned in the body of it, yet we can perfectly well understand why it is called "A Psalm of Solomon."

SAMUEL: Let me repeat that point we made last time: when we speak of "A Psalm of David," that doesn't necessarily mean a psalm *authored* by David.

VAN DOREN:    No, it may also mean a psalm *about* David.

SAMUEL:    "About," or "concerning," or "having to do with" or possibly "in the style of" David. Some translations have rendered the heading of this particular Psalm 72 as *"for* Solomon."

VAN DOREN:    The final verse in Psalm 72, as we've noted, says: "The prayers of David the son of Jesse are ended," so we know that David here is supposed to be praying to God in behalf of a son of his who will be king. That is quite explicit, wouldn't you say?

SAMUEL:    Oh, yes!

VAN DOREN:    It's fascinating to see just how explicit the prayer becomes—at one point particularly —the point of judgment or justice. We all know, of course, the famous stories of Solomon's wisdom as a judge, once he became king. Well, it's as if that had been anticipated here:

> *Give the king Thy judgments, O God,*
> *And Thy righteousness unto the king's son;*
> *That he may judge Thy people with righteousness,*
> *And Thy poor with justice.*

PSALM
72:1–11

I want to underline the word "poor" right there at the beginning of the psalm, because it will be the keyword of the entire psalm.

> *Let the mountains bear peace to the people,*
> *And the hills, through righteousness.*
> *May he judge the poor of the people,*

*And save the children of the needy,*
*And crush the oppressor.*
*They shall fear Thee while the sun endureth,*
*And so long as the moon, throughout all generations.*
*May he come down like rain upon the mown grass,*
*As showers that water the earth.*
*In his days let the righteous flourish,*
*And abundance of peace, till the moon be no more.*

*May he have dominion also from sea to sea,*
*And from the River*[22] *unto the ends of the earth.*
*Let them that dwell in the wilderness bow before him;*
*And his enemies lick the dust.*
*The kings of Tarshish and of the isles shall render tribute;*
*The kings of Sheba and Seba shall offer gifts.*
*Yea, all kings shall prostrate themselves before him;*
*All nations shall serve him.*

But then, here's the interesting thing for me: this great
splendor he wants for his son—splendor which might
suggest an oriental potentate who has no regard for
anything except his own grandeur—suddenly it turns
out to be a splendor *so that* he shall be a just judge in
behalf of the poor:

PSALM            *For he will deliver the needy when he crieth;*
72:12–15

You see, that will be the final sign of his greatness.

*The poor also, and him that hath no helper.*
*He will have pity on the poor and needy,*
*And the souls of the needy he will save:*
*He will redeem their soul from oppression and violence,*
*And precious will their blood be in his sight;*
*That they may live, and that he may give them of the gold of*
*    Sheba,*
*That they may pray for him continually,*
*Yea, bless him all the day.*

I merely wanted to point out how the very heart of that psalm has to do with the justice of Solomon. By the way, the psalm prays for power as an attribute of Solomon, but the real thing that it prays for is justice—and justice for the poor.

SAMUEL:    Two thoughts occurred to me while you were reading. The first is that if we take this as being the testament left by David for his son, it stands in a certain contrast to what we read in the historical books, that is, in the narrative of David's life. At the end of his life, when he called in Solomon to acknowledge that he was about to depart this life, and that Solomon was to be king, he gave his son certain instructions that stick in our craw, as we say. David wanted revenge taken on those who had insulted or see I KINGS opposed him in the course of his earlier life. And 2:5–9 somehow, this is so incongruous with what we would think of the old man David, who had lived this long and rich life, still bearing a grudge! I often take this psalm as being the offset; that what he actually said to his son, what he *meant* to say to him, the real, permanent testament that he left to him was contained in this psalm: "This is the purpose of your kingship."

The second thought goes away from the biblical text and biblical tradition. You suggested before that he asks for power. Now, of course, power is a very dangerous thing.

VAN DOREN:    Probably *the* most dangerous thing!

SAMUEL:   Yes, it's more dangerous than hunger, more dangerous than greed, except in the sense that, sometimes, greed is associated with the desire for power. What I was thinking of was how this strain crept not only into the Western world at large, but into the pagan world. There are echoes of this prayer for justice and for power in Vergil's vision of a just Roman empire—it's in his *Aeneid.*[23] Of course, the Roman empire didn't become just.

VAN DOREN:   No, it did not.

SAMUEL:   It became corrupt, which is the power that you were speaking about.

VAN DOREN:   There never was such a thing as a just empire, I'm afraid.

SAMUEL:   We dream about it. Dante dreamed about it in the Middle Ages, and I suppose the British, in building their empire, thought of spreading the doctrine of cricket and fair play to all the races of the world. But there's no way, ultimately, of reconciling power with justice. The very fact that you have power is in itself an injustice.

Now I think we can lead here from David as the representative of the people, the great Jewish figure, to the whole historical background of the psalms. They echo and reecho with historical references, and a consciousness of the *people* playing a role in the world—not just as individuals. I'd like to dwell on that for a moment, Mark. The peculiarity (as it seems to me and to others) of the Jewish religion as a whole is that what we have here is a *people* dedicated —not simply individuals who have seen the light and are good people—a *people* organized for the purpose of fulfilling God's will.

VAN DOREN:    Well, organized by the very thought of God Himself, because that is the principle of organization, is it not? I mean, Jewish history as the Book of Psalms remembers it, or as the psalms create it (if that's what they're doing) is the history of the people and of the people's God. And the relations between them consisted—as we have said before[24]— of their alternately remembering and forgetting Him. Psalm 78 is a recapitulation of those dreadful moments of history in which the people forgot their God— forgot what He had done for them, forgot not only what they had promised Him, but what He had promised them. It's a record of their backslidings, their stumblings. The psalm begins:

> *Give ear, O my people, to my teaching;*
> *Incline your ears to the words of my mouth.*
> *I will open my mouth with a parable;*
> *I will utter dark sayings concerning days of old.*

PSALM
78:1–2

SAMUEL    *(interrupting):*  What a beautiful phrase that is, "dark sayings"! I wonder whether he means "difficult to understand," or "oppressive on the heart"?

VAN DOREN:    I would guess "difficult to understand," because there's nothing more difficult

for any people than its own past. You know, any
people has great difficulty remembering its past, and
holding itself up to some standards that the past suggests.

SAMUEL:    It may be that you are right. You
remember that famous saying of Hegel's: "What experience and history teach is this: that people and gov-
ernments never have learnt anything from history, or
acted on principles deduced from it."[25] So it is perhaps
that baffled feeling: "Look, we know what there has
been—it's been told; but we don't understand how to
make use of it!"

VAN DOREN:    But every institution, every nation for that matter, has a dreadful tendency to run
down. And every such body has memories of some
good days, some original days, some first days, in
which somehow, the truth was understood. The people of our nation are told every day to remember the
Founding Fathers. And members of any profession are
asked to remember the great old doctors, the great old
lawyers. . . .

SAMUEL:    I think that's a sound attitude. You
remember, there was a time in America—the great
"debunking" era or epoch, or whatever it was called
—when it was the fashion to say about the Founding
Fathers, "Well, yes, they were able men, but each one
was pursuing his own selfish purposes, and what has
emerged happens to be good." I don't like that attitude for this reason: if the good of a man survives,
forget what he did from selfish motives. He left a

creative heritage, and that is the thing that we have to concentrate on.

VAN DOREN:    Yes. The reason that I continue to believe that the medical profession is somehow in a good state is that every June, when doctors are graduated from medical schools, they are asked to stand and listen to the Oath of Hippocrates, the great old doctor who understood the principles of the art. He wrote that oath, and it remains true. It remains difficult also to support in one's practice. His oath today might be regarded as "dark sayings concerning days of old" —the idea of "darkness" referring to the difficulty of digging out these facts from the past.

SAMUEL:    Or interpreting them for our own use.

VAN DOREN:    And thoroughly understanding them. Let me go back now to the psalm:

*I will utter dark sayings concerning days of old.*                    PSALM
*That which we have heard and known,*                         78:2–8
*And our fathers have told us,*
*We will not hide from their children,*
*Telling to the generation to come the praises of the Lord,*
*And His strength, and His wondrous works that He hath*
  *done.*

*For He established a testimony in Jacob,*
*And appointed a law in Israel,*
*Which He commanded our fathers,*
*That they should make them known to their children;*
*That the generation to come might know them, even the chil-*
  *dren that should be born;*
*Who should arise and tell them to their children,*

*That they might put their confidence in God,*
*And not forget the works of God,*
*But keep His commandments;*
*And might not be as their fathers,*
*A stubborn and rebellious generation;*
*A generation that set not their heart aright,*
*And whose spirit was not stedfast with God.*

Then the rest of Psalm 78 is a story of the ups and downs with respect to this principle. The people sometimes remembered, sometimes forgot, sometimes doubted and sometimes rebelled. For example:

PSALM
78:53–56

*And He led them safely, and they feared not;*
*But the sea overwhelmed their enemies.*
*And He brought them to His holy border, . . .*
*Yet they tried and provoked God, the Most High,*
*And kept not His testimonies; . . .*

And of course, there comes the awful moment at Sinai, when Moses, descending from the mountain, finds the people already worshiping the Golden Calf.

SAMUEL:    Mark, let me ask you: Do you know of any other people that has left a monument in poetry for all mankind to read—a monument of its sins of the past?

VAN DOREN:    No! I've said that before on other occasions, and I'm delighted to have a chance to say it again. *That,* maybe, is the ultimate distinction of the Bible: it is a perfect record, not only of the glory of this people's past, but also of the inglory. Its complete frankness is marvelous!

SAMUEL:    I often think that Germany will not be redeemed until there's a tremendous monument in every city: "The shame of Germany: the time of Hitler."

VAN DOREN:    That's right!

# V

## REMEMBERING THE PAST

SAMUEL:   We closed our last talk, Mark, with some reflections on the willingness of the Jewish people as a people—and this is a unique characteristic—to remember its corporate sins. As you said, the Bible is remarkable for its complete frankness in recording both the glory and the inglory. This occurs very often in Jewish liturgy, too. One of the most famous prayers of the Jews is the corporate confession uttered on Yom Kippur, the Day of Atonement. It's a long list of all possible human sins. The people stand up and they say: *"Ashamnu, bagadnu, gazalnu. . . .* We have sinned, we have betrayed, we have robbed. . . ." The confession is put in Hebrew alphabetical order,[26] and the authors find a sin for every letter. There isn't a single sin that they don't cover in that fashion, and the congregation says it *for the people.* It's not, *"I* have sinned," but the entire congregation saying in unison, "Somewhere among us, the sin has been committed. *We* are guilty, and therefore, *we* ask for forgiveness." I was thinking of this as you recalled Psalm 78, which has to do with the historical consciousness of the Jewish people.

VAN DOREN:  I was reading about the stubborn and rebellious generation which had been succeeded by generations not stubborn and rebellious. And yet, lo and behold, they became so again! The Psalmist has rehearsed some of the marvelous things God did for His people in the Wilderness, but then the people start murmuring again:

> *Yet went they on still to sin against Him,*
> *To rebel against the Most High in the desert.*
> *And they tried God in their heart*
> *By asking food for their craving.*
> *Yea, they spoke against God;*
> *They said: "Can God prepare a table in the wilderness?*
> *Behold, He smote the rock that waters gushed out,*
> *And streams overflowed;*
> *Can He give bread also?*
> *Or will He provide flesh for His people?"*
> *Therefore the Lord heard, and was wroth;*
> *And a fire was kindled against Jacob,*
> *And anger also went up against Israel;*
> *Because they believed not in God,*
> *And trusted not in His salvation.*

PSALM
78:17–22

That is to say, they had spoken in scorn and in sarcasm, as if to say, "Of course, this can't be done!" They had not believed that He was all-powerful, and He was angry because they doubted Him. There follows a

long recital in that psalm of their punishment, and then
we hear:

PSALM
78:38–39

> *But He, being full of compassion, forgiveth iniquity, and*
>     *destroyeth not;*
> *Yea, many a time doth He turn His anger away,*
> *And doth not stir up all His wrath.*
> *So He remembered that they were but flesh;*
> *A wind that passeth away, and cometh not again.*

SAMUEL:   That's a very beautiful thing!

VAN DOREN:   Yes, and it's very important
that that is there.

SAMUEL:   This variation in mood is one of the
captivating things about biblical texts. When people
speak of "contradictions" in the Bible, they forget—
as I've often noted—that with small people, contradictions cancel out; with great people, contradictions
add up. They become something affirmative. Here in
the psalms, there is this remembrance of the sins of the
Jewish people, but in the Prophets—say in Jeremiah—there is the recollection of the time in the past
when the Jewish people seemed to be perfect. The
Prophet says, speaking for God to the Jewish people:

JER. 2:2

> *I remember for thee the affection of thy youth;*
> *The love of thine espousals;*
> *How thou wentest after Me in the wilderness,*
> *In a land that was not sown.*

There is in that such a tender gratitude for the faith
that the people had in God: "Thou wentest after Me
in the wilderness. . . ." At that point, He forgets com-

pletely other episodes in which He was furious with them—for example, the time when He told the people through unnamed prophets: "You have done evil and provoked Me since the day your fathers left Egypt!" And for that reason, He says, "I will wipe Jerusalem as a man wipeth a dish, wiping it and turning it upside down!" You have these alternations of mood which are, in my opinion, a reflection of the vicissitudes of history: the alternating good fortune and evil fortune. It is correct to chide the people, and it is correct to comfort the people. There is no contradiction in doing both.

*see* II KINGS 21:10–15

VAN DOREN: No contradiction, because if there seems to be any, it is resolved in God's knowledge—which the Bible so wisely never forgets to express—that men are, after all, men. They are not God, like Him. They are not like Him at all, except insofar as they resemble Him through the gift that He gave them to resemble Him. But they are flesh, a passing wind, they are impermanent creatures. Men are the only creatures to whom He gave intellect, heart, understanding, and the power to understand Him. But it isn't a thing that He seems to understand; He seems to believe that He can expect them to hold in perfection.

SAMUEL: No! The very function of free will implies that you're going to sin. If you have free will and you're never going to sin, it's a fake free will. And therefore it is perfectly human—no, it's *more* than human, it has a divine wisdom about it—that the two alternations of mood are accepted and resolved in the end.

VAN DOREN:   Yes, and maybe the mercy of God consists of nothing so much as in His power always to remember the limitations of men. He does not expect the impossible from them.

SAMUEL:   Contrast that Psalm 78—which is one of the historical psalms, if we can so classify it— with another, Psalm 114, where the recollection of the coming out from Egypt is one great burst of joy and of enthusiasm:

PSALM 114

*When Israel came forth out of Egypt,*
*The house of Jacob from a people of strange language;*
*Judah became His sanctuary,*
*Israel His dominion.*

*The sea saw it, and fled;*
*The Jordan turned backward.*
*The mountains skipped like rams,*
*The hills like young sheep.*

*What aileth thee, O thou sea, that thou fleest?*
*Thou Jordan, that thou turnest backward?*
*Ye mountains, that ye skip like rams;*
*Ye hills, like young sheep?*

*Tremble, thou earth, at the presence of the Lord,*
*At the presence of the God of Jacob;*
*Who turned the rock into a pool of water,*
*The flint into a fountain of waters.*

*see* NUM. 20:11–12

What is amazing about that closing passage is this: Moses' striking of the rock to bring forth water at Kadesh was an occasion of *sin*. Moses and Aaron were both rebuked and were denied the privilege of being admitted finally into the Promised Land. The legends expand on the guilt of Moses in losing his temper with a rock![27] He insulted that harmless, quiet, and guiltless thing by striking it, when he could have spoken to it. But here in Psalm 114, it's made an occasion of great rejoicing: "Who turned the rock into a pool of water,/ The flint into a fountain of waters." This again is the reflection of changes in historic mood.

VAN DOREN: There's a change in mood between Psalm 78 and Psalm 105, too. Psalm 105 is a long account of God's goodness to men, of His perpetual salvation of them, of the covenant He made with Abraham, and with the people later on. There's no reference in it to the failure of the people to keep their part in it, no suggestion of punishment. It's entirely on the affirmative rather than the negative side.

SAMUEL: Again in that same Psalm 105, notice the passage:

> *He opened the rock, and waters gushed out;*
> *They ran, a river in the dry places.*

PSALM
105:41

Actually, Moses split *two* rocks at God's command, one at Horeb and the other at Kadesh, as I just mentioned. This passage omits completely the sinfulness of the people in doubting God's ability to give them water.

*see* EXOD.
17:1–7;
NUM.
20:2–11

VAN DOREN: Psalm 114 is a very powerful short lyric. As a matter of fact, it exerts its power by its very brevity. "When Israel came forth out of Egypt, . . . the sea saw it, and fled, . . . What aileth thee, O

PSALM
114:1,3,5

thou sea . . . ?" In other words, "Sea, didn't you
understand?"

SAMUEL: There's something joyous in it!
"Hey, Sea, what happened to you?" Or, "Mountains,
what's with you?" You know, sometimes to bring this
close to us, you have to suppose a man standing somewhere in New York, saying: "Catskill Mountains,
what has happened to you?" and "Alleghenies, where
are you?"

(laughter)

To the people of biblical times, this was very real. We
often make it purely allusive and abstract by removing
it to a remote past and a remote place.

VAN DOREN: You know, Maurice, we have
thus far referred only to historical psalms. It strikes me
that the word "historical" is not good.

SAMUEL: I agree. I don't think it is, either.

VAN DOREN: I mean by that—and I dare say
you mean, too—we've discussed merely those psalms
which have "dark sayings concerning the days of old,"
and which ask people to remember what is so hard to
remember, our own past. So far, we've referred just
to those psalms that deal with only the creation of man
and his early salvation, the covenant, and the incon-
ceivably dramatic event of the people's coming out of
Egypt and going to the Promised Land. But centuries
go on beyond that in the history recounted in the

Book of Psalms. I don't know myself that any psalm
has ever struck me as being more beautiful or more
wonderful than the psalm which refers, of course, to
a relatively very late historical event, the Babylonian
captivity. That's Psalm 137 which, as we've already
mentioned, could not have been written by David.

SAMUEL: A very Orthodox Jew will always
tell you when you raise this historical objection that
David wrote it prophetically. You can always get
round it that way. But presumably, David did not
write it.

VAN DOREN: Personally, I don't care. I'm
willing to call the psalms "the Psalms of David," and
that, I think, is just a very minor point. Do you agree
that Psalm 137 is particularly beautiful and moving?

SAMUEL: It has what I would call a terrifying
beauty. It has beauty, but there's something also of
horror in it.

VAN DOREN: Oh, of course! I understood
that. I think, by the way, that is always latent in any of
these great poems, as perhaps it must be latent in every
great poem everywhere. Psalm 137 is quite short—
only nine verses, and it's a marvel in view of what it
accomplishes in that brief space. And I'm very glad,
Maurice, that you pointed out that its beauty is something that conquers, or at any rate includes, terror.
The people are understood in this psalm to have been
led away captive, and they're in a land far away where
their captors are contemptuous of them—contemptu-

ous of all their ways, their religion, their rituals, contemptuous even of the songs they sing, even of the
things they like to repeat to one another. The psalm
represents them being insulted in that foreign land by
their captors who, on a certain occasion, say: "Now
sing one of your old songs."

PSALM
137:1-3

*By the rivers of Babylon,*
*There we sat down, yea, we wept,*
*When we remembered Zion.*
*Upon the willows in the midst thereof*
*We hanged up our harps.*
*For there they that led us captive asked of us words of song,*
*And our tormentors asked of us mirth:*
*"Sing us one of the songs of Zion."*

The command to sing is uttered in complete contempt,
wouldn't you say so, Maurice?

SAMUEL:    Yes! The captors are saying, "Sing
us one of your Jew songs!" That's what it really comes
to.

VAN DOREN:    "One of your silly old songs
that you take so seriously." And the psalm continues
with the question:

PSALM
137:4-9

*How shall we sing the Lord's song*
*In a foreign land?*
*If I forget thee, O Jerusalem,*
*Let my right hand forget her cunning.*
*Let my tongue cleave to the roof of my mouth,*
*If I remember thee not;*
*If I set not Jerusalem*
*Above my chiefest joy.*

*Remember, O Lord, against the children of Edom*
*The day of Jerusalem;*

*Who said: "Raze it, raze it,*
*Even to the foundation thereof."*
*O daughter of Babylon, that art to be destroyed;*
*Happy shall he be, that repayeth thee*
*As thou hast served us.*
*Happy shall he be, that taketh and dasheth thy little ones*
*Against the rock.*

SAMUEL:   That is a terrible ending, isn't it?[28]

VAN DOREN:   Yes, terrible as other things have been in that psalm, too.

SAMUEL:   I've heard Jews speak of that ending with distaste, even with fear, saying: "Don't you think we ought to omit that from the Psalter?" or "Let's pass over it." My feeling has been that it would be wrong. This is a historical record, and this is how the people felt. This is how many Jewish people must have felt in the Hitler time, when hundreds of thousands were being sent into the gas chambers, and their cry of pain—a pain that was intolerable—went out, "Destroy them, God!" And it would be wrong to have that forgotten. This is an expression of the anguish of a people:

*Happy shall he be, that taketh and dasheth thy little ones*
*Against the rock.*

There were Jews who felt that way, as Jews have felt in our days about the Nazis.

VAN DOREN:   Well, of course!

SAMUEL:   And then it passes away! And that it shouldn't be on the record—make it appear a sweet and uniform and unstained record—is not the way of the Bible. In fact, this in itself is one of these records in which the people has put down for perpetuity: "This is how we felt at the time, and it would be wrong to say that we didn't feel that way."

VAN DOREN:   That is what I've tried to say many times in these conversations, Maurice. Think of David himself, of whom we were speaking in some of our past talks. What if the story of David, as we find it in the two Books of Samuel, had been edited so that every failure of his, every falling away from the ideal which he understood so well, had been expunged from the record? In the first place, we wouldn't believe him, probably, but in the second place, I doubt if he would interest us very much, because we wouldn't know the depth to which he could be tempted, the depth to which he could fall from a very high place. You see, he always returned to that high place, and his position then—the aspect he presents to us then—is all the more moving because he has ascended again.

SAMUEL:   You know, Arnold J. Toynbee's *A Study of History* suggests that it would have been an "improvement" to have excluded from the Bible the Books of Samuel and of Kings, as well as Joshua and Judges because they are so full of blood and of human sin. Toynbee recalls that Ulfilas, the apostle of the Goths back in the fourth century, who made the first translation of the Bible into a Teutonic language, "wisely omitted the Books of Samuel and Kings, on the ground that war and bloodshed were too much in the minds of the Goths as it was, without their proclivity in this direction being consecrated and confirmed by the authority of the sacred book of their new religion."[29] Toynbee goes on to say: "It is a pity that Luther and the English translators did not follow Ulfilas's example, or, indeed, improve on it by omitting Joshua and Judges as well!" This emasculation of the Bible—because that's what it amounts to—would simply leave us without a Bible.

VAN DOREN: Yes!

SAMUEL: Then it would be merely a tract.

VAN DOREN: A tract, and a very tame one, and a very unconvincing one!

SAMUEL: Let me give you another instance of passages that some people would delete from the Passover *Haggadah,* the story of the Exodus from Egypt, which consists largely of portions taken from the text of the Hebrew Bible. Toward the end of the Passover *seder,* there's a very curious ceremony. Everybody at the *seder* table has a wine cup; and there is always a cup or goblet filled for the prophet Elijah, which nobody drinks, of course. After the meal and the grace, the door is opened for Elijah, everyone stands, and the following passages are read in Hebrew:

> *Pour out Thy wrath upon the nations that know Thee not,*
> *And upon the kingdoms that call not upon Thy Name.*
> *For they have devoured Jacob*
> *And laid waste his abode.*

PSALM
79:6–7

*Pour out Thy rage upon them, let Thy fury overtake them.*

*Pursue them with the breath of Thy fury,*

*And destroy them from under the heavens of the Lord.*

And then, quietly, they say, *"Baruch ha-ba"* ("Welcome"), meaning the prophet Elijah has just entered. Now the background to this has sometimes been given as follows: in the Middle Ages, the Jews were accused of using human blood to make their Passover matzos. These accusations brought on terrible slaughters, persecutions, and trials over the centuries. (Indeed, there was a world-famous trial of a Jew in Czarist Russia on this monstrous and false charge on the eve of World War I.)[30] It is thought in some quarters that Jews began the custom of opening the door at the *seder* in the Middle Ages in order to tell all the nations, "Come in and see if we've used any blood!" They used the occasion to make that remark, "Pour out Thy wrath." That was the kind of welcome they gave to these putative visitors who came in with this accusation. Now the removal of this from the Passover *Haggadah*—the book used at the *seder* to tell the story of Passover—is to me a very deep error. Two groups in modern Jewish religious life, Reform Judaism and the Reconstructionists, have removed it, and I think that they are mistaken. The passage should be there because in this is imbedded Jewish suffering and Jewish history. We mustn't forget history; we must transcend it.

VAN DOREN: Yes, of course. We must never try to remove out of the past those painful things from which we've learned so much, because we do learn from pain and suffering, as everybody knows. Oh, I

quite agree with you, and I detect a tendency everywhere these days to do that with almost everything—
not only in the world of religion, but elsewhere, too.
We try to forget things that we should not forget, that
we really cannot forget, but only pretend that we
can.

SAMUEL:   By the way, Mark, in this Psalm 137
—and in many others, too—there are passages in
which something is lost in translation in spite of the
greatness of the English translation. Reading this
psalm in English, you would say to yourself, "It
couldn't be better!" It is so powerful that you say,
"Well, I don't care. The Hebrew may be very beautiful, but how can you have a more powerful expression
than 'If I forget thee, O Jerusalem, let my right hand
forget her cunning'?" Now the Hebrew is just two
words: *"Tishcakh yemini,* let my right hand forget itself." The meaning is: let it have no more memory of
what it was able to do.

VAN DOREN:   That's wonderful!

SAMUEL:   Of course, it's very beautiful to say,
"Let my right hand forget her cunning." I wouldn't
like to have it said, "Forget her ability," or "Forget
her craft," or "Let me be unable to use my right
hand." "Cunning" is the proper phrase.[31]

VAN DOREN:   "Cunning," of course, meant
originally "craft."

SAMUEL:   Yes, "being able."

VAN DOREN:   "Ability."

SAMUEL:   It's   connected   with   the   word
"king," I believe.

VAN DOREN:   No, the derivation is from the
Old English *cunnan,* "to know" or "to be able." The
word "king" is from the Old English *cyning.* The Old
English *cennan,* meaning "to make known," "to declare" or "proclaim," is still with us in the word "ken"
—you know, something is within your "ken." However, now that we're speaking about Psalm 137, how
do you understand the question, "How shall we sing
the Lord's song in a foreign land?" Is it rhetorical?
Then, "If I forget thee, O Jerusalem . . . ." In other
words, is the implication clear that they did *not* sing
the song?

SAMUEL:   Yes, of course! You've got at it.
The point is, the people refuse to sing; but they add,
"It isn't because we've forgotten it!"

VAN DOREN:   No, of course not.

SAMUEL:   You see, the captors said: "Sing us
one of the songs of Zion." The captives reply, "We
haven't forgotten it, but we won't sing. How shall we
sing the Lord's song in a foreign land?" And then it
goes on, "If I forget thee, O Jerusalem, et cetera." It's
a rhetorical question, and a contemptuous reply.

VAN DOREN:   So the whole passage means:
"How could we have sung that song there? Not that

we have forgotten it, because if ever I forget thee, O Jerusalem, let my right hand . . . ." That's how important *that* consideration is: "Let my tongue cleave to the roof of my mouth if I remember thee not, if I set not Jerusalem above my chiefest joy. But in *that* time and place, among those people, without the Temple about us, and without all the accompaniments of our song, we had to be speechless." Is that what you understand?

SAMUEL:   Yes! And it is remarkable how this echoes into the present, and gathers volume with a grisly reminder of what modern tormentors did to Jews. Before the world wars, for example, the Polish *pan,* or lord, or landowner, might torment the Jews on his estate. If he'd been drinking and was high, he'd make the Jews come before him and sing and dance. And on many occasions, the Nazis compelled the Jews to take the *Torah* scrolls into their arms and dance about for the delectation of the tormentors. This is what is said in Psalm 137: "Our tormentors asked of us mirth: 'Sing us one of the songs of Zion!'" I remember a story told of Palestine back in 1924–25, when a British soldier under the Mandate (it's not fair to mention Great Britain at all in this connection!) came down to the Western Wall (the "Wailing Wall") in old Jerusalem. There were some old Jews praying there, but evidently things looked too quiet for him. He threw a coin at one of them and said, "Hey, wail, you blighter, wail!" But getting back to this psalm, there is in it so much misery and so much humiliation that it would be unnatural that it shouldn't end as it does.

VAN DOREN:    Oh, of course! You were speaking last time of the rapid and radical shifts of mood in all of the Bible, but certainly in the Book of Psalms. Let us remember the joy that is expressed in Psalm 126, when the people return home!

SAMUEL:    Yes! I got a little excited on that subject. I'd like to be soothed, as it were, by Psalm 126. It is interpreted as an expression of the captives who were allowed to go back to the homeland after the Babylonian exile, and their prayer that God would now "turn their captivity," or restore their fortunes after the horror of the exile.

VAN DOREN:    I don't think you got too excited! But it's also well to remember the intense excitement of joy when they return:

PSALM 126    *When the Lord brought back those that returned to Zion,*
*We were like unto them that dream.*

What a line that is—"We couldn't believe it!"

*Then was our mouth filled with laughter,*
*And our tongue with singing;*
*Then said they among the nations:*
*"The Lord hath done great things with these."*
*The Lord hath done great things with us;*
*We are rejoiced.*
*Turn our captivity, O Lord,*
*As the streams in the dry land.*
*They that sow in tears*
*Shall reap in joy.*
*Though he goeth on his way weeping that beareth the measure*
    *of seed,*
*He shall come home with joy, bearing his sheaves.*

SAMUEL: Could anything be lovelier than that phrase, "They that sow in tears shall reap in joy"? The Hebrew is more compact, but not more beautiful: *Ha-zor'im b'dim'ah b'rinah yik'tsoru.* There is a mirror of life there: "Bear with the hard time, and the good time will come after it."

# VI

# IN PRAISE OF THE LAW

VAN DOREN: Well, where shall we go from the historical psalms, Maurice?

SAMUEL: We can go into a dozen things. Since we were speaking of the conscience of the people, I think that the historical would lead us into an examination of the sense of the Law—that is to say, the *Torah*—and of justice that dominates the psalms. It would be important at this point, I think, to see how the psalms interpret the concepts of Law and of goodness, and how we find in them a continuous singing of the praises of the Law.

VAN DOREN: That reminds me of something which has struck me most forcefully in these psalms

which refer to the Law—what that term, "the Law,"
meant and still means to the Jews. There's a richness
in that term: it condenses volumes and universes of
meaning. In the very first psalm, suddenly the term is
mentioned—and as a lovely thing! It is not among
every people that the Law is thought of in that way.
Remember how the psalm begins:

> *Happy is the man that hath not walked in the counsel of the*     PSALM
>     *wicked,*                                                      1:1–2
> *Nor stood in the way of sinners,*
> *Nor sat in the seat of the scornful.*
> *But his delight is in the law of the Lord;*
> *And in His law doth he meditate day and night.*

There's a kind of almost luxurious feeling: the Law is
something terribly good—not merely to think about
or to remember, but good to have, good even to *eat!*

SAMUEL *(laughing):*   He revels in the Law!

VAN DOREN:   He *rolls* in the Law!

SAMUEL:   Yes, what a curious concept, when
the Law is taken in its literal and constricted sense!

VAN DOREN:   There's another passage that I
want to come to later, which suddenly bursts forth,     PSALM
"Oh how love I Thy law!" But in this present context,     119: 97
the first psalm goes on:

> *And he shall be like a tree planted by streams of water,*     PSALM 1:3
> *That bringeth forth its fruit in its season,*
> *And whose leaf doth not wither;*
> *And in whatsoever he doeth he shall prosper.*

The suggestion there is of something that is good for you in more senses than the law (to use that term in its everyday secular sense) ordinarily is supposed to be good for you. I'd love to know something more about the full meaning in the biblical sense of that wonderful word "Law."

SAMUEL: The English word "law" is used to translate the Hebrew term *torah,* but it is far from satisfactory. Strictly speaking, *torah* means "teaching" or "guidance"; it's connected with the Hebrew word *moreh,* namely, "a teacher." But the *Torah* is also the name given to the Pentateuch, the Five Books of Moses; and carrying it still further, *Torah* in addition refers to *all* of Jewish learning and all of sacred literature. When a Jew is said to be "studying *Torah,*" he may be concentrating on the Pentateuch, but it's more likely that he's ranging through all the commentaries, all the sacred books, all the scholars, ancient and modern. Carrying the meaning of *Torah* even beyond this, in its very broadest sense the term means "a way of life," or "This is the law of your life." I've just touched on an approximation of what has accumulated over centuries and centuries *upon* the word, rather than *in* it. The word is loaded with all sorts of meanings, recollections, and echoes of martyrdom for what Jews suffered for this particular way of living. The strictly close word for a "law" in Hebrew is *chok;* that's an enactment, a regulation. *Torah* is far wider than any word can convey in the English language.

VAN DOREN: Yes, I was going to say, Maurice, that certainly it is loaded beyond the point where

you would think that it meant "statutes" or "enact-
ments" or "laws," as we often use the word, in the
plural. I'm sure that it means, among other things,
memories of happiness that had been achieved by
those who somehow, as we say, "knew" how to live.
In the Greek and Roman world, there was a virtue
sometimes called *prudentia,* sometimes called "wisdom." Our word "prudence" comes from *prudentia.*
The ancient word was trying to refer to this whole
body of understanding, which is indescribable.

SAMUEL: Yes, but *prudentia* was used in the
sense of *worldly* wisdom—how to get along with *people,*
rather than embracing also one's relationship to God.
I was going to remark before, Mark, that there are
certain words in Hebrew (and they have become part
of the Yiddish language, too) which are untranslatable
because all of the associations which inhere in them
now can be known only by the people who have
known and *felt* the history in them. Take a word like
"exile." In the Yiddish, it's pronounced *golus;* in the
Hebrew, it's pronounced *galut.* I prefer the pronuncia-
tion *golus,* which is used outside of the State of Israel,
because this word—"exile" is the only translation for
it—has in Yiddish, so to speak, a "library effect." It's
not a word, it's not a book, it is a *library* of the experience of the Jewish people. When a Jew says that something is "as interminable as the Exile," you know and
he knows what he's referring to. "Exile" in English
means that you are sent into a foreign land, you're
alienated from a given circumstance . . . .

VAN DOREN: For a while.

SAMUEL:   . . . For a while, yes; and even if exiled for life, it's just for *your* life. Here in the word *golus* is an exile which endured two thousand years, and the word has taken on that weight. Similarly, the word *Torah* must be seen as carrying with it all the experience of thousands of years, and all of the willingness of the Jew to return to it, even if he has defected from it, and to see in it *the* consolation and joy of being.

VAN DOREN:   Well now, that joy of being is what I keep noticing as I read through the psalms which have to do with the Law. In Psalm 19, the Psalmist who, you might think, has been talking about something else altogether—namely, the beauty of the entire universe and its power to express the existence and the goodness of God—suddenly breaks off after verse 7 and begins again. But I think there's nothing inconsistent in it:

PSALM
19:8–11

*The law of the Lord is perfect, restoring the soul;*
*The testimony of the Lord is sure, making wise the simple.*
*The precepts of the Lord are right, rejoicing the heart;*
*The commandment of the Lord is pure, enlightening the eyes.*
*The fear of the Lord is clean, enduring for ever;*
*The ordinances of the Lord are true, they are righteous altogether;*
*More to be desired are they than gold, yea, than much fine gold;*
*Sweeter also than honey and the honeycomb.*

The words "sweet," "fine," and "desire" have a touch almost of the sensuous there.

SAMUEL:   Yes. That reminds me of a popular Yiddish folk song in which the Jew is singing, "The peasant goes into the inn and grabs himself a glass of whiskey. The Jew goes into the house of study and grabs himself a page of *Mishnah,"* which would be translated in this particular context as "a page of learning." It's such an odd expression, *khapt er dort a mishnayesl arayn!* Here's a man, an ordinary Jew, a workingman, thinking of a page of learning—that is, the study of the *Torah*—as being something you get hold of. You swallow it, and it goes down like a hot blintz! *(laughing)* Now imagine, let us say, two other workingmen, ordinary men, one saying to the other, "Hey, Bill, let's go and grab a page of Shakespeare!" It just doesn't belong at all!

Now this delight in the *Torah* as a fulfillment goes through you, and it has all of the possibilities that a human being needs, like the manna in the desert. The Bible tells us that the taste of the manna was like the coriander seed, whatever that is; but actually, the legends say that it tasted like anything you wanted.[32] There was a particular reason why the Jews were sinful in rebelling against the manna, because *anyhow* it tasted like meat, or—God forbid! it may even have tasted like *pork* without their knowing it! But it was supposed to have tasted like anything at all. Now the *Torah* has everything in it that a man needs; one might even say that it has the physical fulfillments for a man. But I want to go back to Psalm 19, which you were citing just now, Mark. You remarked on the curious contrast between the first part of it, which apparently has nothing to do with the Law itself, and the last part, which has an entirely different note.

*see* EXOD. 16:31; NUM. 11:7–8

VAN DOREN:   I was saying I found nothing inconsistent between the two parts. I think there is a

transition that we can understand. But certainly, in the
first part, the word "law" is not mentioned at all. The
psalm begins in the very sky itself:

PSALM          *The heavens declare the glory of God,*
19:2–7         *And the firmament showeth His handiwork;*
               *Day unto day uttereth speech,*
               *And night unto night revealeth knowledge;*
               *There is no speech, there are no words,*
               *Neither is their voice heard.*
               *Their line is gone out through all the earth,*
               *And their words to the end of the world.*
               *In them hath He set a tent for the sun,*
               *Which is as a bridegroom coming out of his chamber,*
               *And rejoiceth as a strong man to run his course.*
               *His going forth is from the end of the heaven,*
               *And his circuit unto the ends of it;*
               *And there is nothing hid from the heat thereof.*

And then we have:

PSALM 19:8     *The law of the Lord is perfect, restoring the soul;* . . .

Well now, I think the suggestion at the beginning had
been that "day unto day uttereth speech, and night
unto night revealeth knowledge"—and yet without
words. You see, the Psalmist says: "I don't mean that
day *talks* to day, but their line goes out through all the
earth, and their words to the end of the world." That
is, the *truth* goes out to the end of the world. *Torah,*
or Law, could mean for me nothing less than the whole
truth.

SAMUEL:   Yes! That is why Psalm 19 has a sort
of counterpoint, I think: beginning with the harmony
of the universe as a whole, the Psalmist plunges from

the supreme heights into human affairs, and says: "All these things are one!" Hence, "meditating on the Law" doesn't mean considering it simply human relations (I don't mean to belittle it at all); but considering it the entire context of human relations—all the universe, its harmony and its perfections are reflected in what human beings should think of in connection with each other.

VAN DOREN:   That reminds me, Maurice, of our attempt once[33] when we were discussing the Wisdom Books of the Bible to pin down that word "wisdom"; and our final discovery—if it was a discovery; it was for me at any rate—was that the word somehow referred to the knowledge of *everything*. It was not limited solely to precepts only, magnificent and necessary as they might be, but encompassed the understanding of the entire structure of the world, from the beginning on. All nature, somehow or other, would be consistent with the Law, all history, all truth, naturally, would have to be consistent. By "wisdom" the writers of the Wisdom Books, and of the entire Bible, meant literally *all* of the truth—truth that a scientist, or a poet, or a philosopher might discover. . . .

SAMUEL:   Yes! To the Jew, all knowledge belonged to the *Torah*.

VAN DOREN:   It was not irrelevant.

SAMUEL:   It mingled in a single, consistent whole. This is reflected in parts of Psalm 119, as you mentioned earlier. Psalm 119 is very long and very ingenious. In Hebrew, it's in the form of an acrostic, each stanza and each verse within that stanza beginning with a letter of the Hebrew alphabet in sequence, from the first letter, *alef,* to the last, *tav.* You specifically cited verse 97.

VAN DOREN:   Yes, at verse 97, the Psalmist once more breaks out in adoration of the Law:

PSALM
119:97–100

*Oh how love I Thy law!*
*It is my meditation all the day.*
*Thy commandments make me wiser than mine enemies;*
*For they are ever with me.*
*I have more understanding than all my teachers;*
*For Thy testimonies are my meditation.*
*I understand more than mine elders,*
*Because I have kept Thy precepts.*

SAMUEL:   This illustrates what you were implying before. The Psalmist says, "I understand more than mine elders because I have kept Thy precepts". What might sound like a rather arrogant remark is actually this: "If I obey the Law" (which means, in part, "If I keep on dwelling on these subjects") "then I'm fulfilled. My teachers can't give me anything. It's the Law that gives it to me—the *Torah,* or wisdom, or the totality of knowledge."

VAN DOREN:   And of course, something very great is being referred to here, and is being invoked; namely, the understanding that the ultimate authority is the truth, the authority which both elders and ourselves must submit to—the thing that both priests and teachers, and ourselves, are subject to, something greater than both of us is the truth, whatever it is. And the suggestion here for me is that if I love the Law enough, and if I meditate upon it day and night, and thoroughly understand it, and if I'm perfect in it—and I suppose one cannot quite be perfect in it—nevertheless, if I am, then I understand more than all my teachers, because I've understood it by myself.

SAMUEL: Something else flows from this, too, Mark, and that is: if the Law has this immense connotation, then judgment is not the dreadful thing that it is sometimes regarded as. Now here and there you will meet in the Hebrew Bible the concept of the judgment as taking place on a great and terrible day, before which men tremble. But predominantly in the Book of Psalms, you've noticed that the word "judgment" has a very different tonality, haven't you?

VAN DOREN: Oh, yes. It is something that is sought for, and longed for, as if it were absent or hard to get. Yes, one hopes that the day will come when judgment is somehow available, as if it were bound to be a good thing. The meaning of "judgment" here shouldn't be confused with the word "justice" as we ordinarily use it, when we say, for example: "All I want is justice!" We usually mean by that, "I want judgment on my side!" don't we?

SAMUEL: Yes! *(laughing)* That's one of the great cant phrases of the world, "All I'm looking for is justice!"

VAN DOREN: Yes, but what the Psalmist wants is judgment to assume operation, judgment to be once more active in the world. He trusts judgment to be right.

SAMUEL: Here again it's the interplay between a people's fate and the individual's fate. The man who was oppressed, or the people which was oppressed, is waiting for judgment; and that wait isn't full of fear and trembling. Knowing that it has been oppressed, the people says: "In the day of judgment, I shall not be afraid. I've suffered so much, let *others* be afraid. I welcome the time!"

But Mark, I'm amused by your reference: "All I want is justice!" Which is what *nobody* in the world wants!

VAN DOREN *(laughing)*: You'd better not ask for it!

SAMUEL: That reminds me of a charming little story I read recently.[34] It's about a woman who used to come to visit a home and say, "I don't want much. Please don't offer me so much food! All I want is a perfect little piece of toast, and a cup of tea, made just so!"—as though she wanted the exquisite exactitude of a great chef to be lavished upon her. "But that's all I want, really. Don't think I'm asking for much!" This is part of the widespread human game of self-deception: "All I want is justice!"

VAN DOREN: I find still another sensation described here in Psalm 119:

*How sweet are Thy words unto my palate!*     PSALM
*Yea, sweeter than honey to my mouth!*        119:103–
104
*From Thy precepts I get understanding;*
*Therefore I hate every false way.*

I find pleasure here, as well as happiness. Do you agree that pleasure is here?

SAMUEL:   Yes, yes, indeed!

VAN DOREN:   There's the wonderful pleasure, in addition to happiness, of knowing somehow what is true, what is right, not through the memorization of precepts, not through the "getting of the Law" (you know, as lawyers sometimes "get law up"); but through an entering into the very spirit of truth. I hope I'm not too abstract in this.

SAMUEL:   No. When a moral problem is resolved in your mind, and for that matter, an intellectual problem, you can say very genuinely, and not at all blasphemously, "Oh God! *That's* the answer!" And there goes through you such a—yes, a *pleasant* feeling: "There *are* answers. What a pleasure!"

VAN DOREN:   I've always remembered a story of the professor of physics at Columbia University who for years had searched for a certain formula. And one day, when he was facing his class and writing on the blackboard, he found it. There it was—and he fainted!

SAMUEL: It reminds me a bit of Archimedes running naked through the streets, shouting, "Eureka!" Or of Schliemann, the great archeologist. It's said that once, when he was examining some cuneiform tablets in the Near East, he suddenly realized that he'd found one of the original stories of the Deluge, predating the Jewish story of the Deluge—and *he* fainted! Now, when one gets an excess of joy and of insight, no wonder that the Psalmist says: "As the hart panteth after the water brooks," and so he pants for a grasp of the Law.

PSALM 42:2

VAN DOREN: Well, you know now, Maurice, you write books—

SAMUEL: I'm not the only one, Mark. I think you've been rather guilty yourself, to the extent of twenty or thirty.

VAN DOREN: I admit it, but that's not the point I'm trying to establish here. You've written books which I greatly admire, and I know very well that there was a stage in the formation of one of those books where you were suddenly happy because you saw it as a book; you saw what the subject was, what the parts of it were. You probably had made a preliminary table of contents. Didn't it please you a great deal to have it suddenly ordered?

SAMUEL *(laughing):* It's a very painful subject, Mark. It's a very fleeting pleasure, and then how often you find that it was a deception, and it never got over. I think with much more satisfaction of the Jewish habit: when a Jew finishes a course of study of pre-scribed length, he says: *Tam ve-nishlam shevach l'El boreh olam* ("It is completed and ended, praise be the Creator of the World"). I've often been relieved to have finished a book. . . .

VAN DOREN: To have finished it, really.

SAMUEL: To get it off. But all the anguish afterward, when you look at it and say, "This is no good! I didn't mean that! That's all wrong! That's where I went off!" I suppose you've felt that, too, haven't you?

VAN DOREN: Oh yes—that feeling, "I could have said it better!"

*(laughter)*

But Maurice, there's one thing that we must make clear to each other, if not to anyone else. I'm sure you will agree with me about this (I'm putting you on the spot now): when the Psalmist speaks his intense, al-most sensuous pleasure, as well as happiness, in some-how being able to live with the Law and meditat-ing upon it, he isn't saying that he is a good and perfect man, is he? He isn't patting himself on the back?

SAMUEL: Oh no! No, no, no!

VAN DOREN: It's terribly important to make that distinction.

SAMUEL: Psalm 119 contains a verse I've often meditated on:

PSALM<br>119:81

*My soul pineth for Thy salvation;*
*In Thy word do I hope.*

You remember that Fra Angelico, before he used to take up the brush every morning to paint, used to say a prayer—and how often I've prayed, too: "I wish I could find the word today!" The Psalmist says:

PSALM<br>119:81–84

*My soul pineth for Thy salvation;*
*In Thy word do I hope.*
*Mine eyes fail for Thy word,*
*Saying: "When wilt Thou comfort me?"*
*For I am become like a wine-skin in the smoke;*[35]
*Yet do I not forget Thy statutes.*
*How many are the days of Thy servant?*
*When wilt Thou execute judgment on them that persecute me?*

This is not the cry of the man self-satisfied in the knowledge that he has acquired wisdom. He feels inadequate, deeply inadequate, and for him, the fulfillment can come only by being filled by the word of God. When that will come, he will realize himself.

VAN DOREN: His happiness is in knowing what goodness does consist of. It may not have anything to do with the complacency on his part in thinking that he has arrived at it, but he knows what it would be if he could achieve it.

SAMUEL: He may never achieve it, but it is the ultimate hope!

VAN DOREN:  Yes, and he lives under that canopy of understanding, which to him is a blessing forever.

SAMUEL:   I suppose it represents for the individual what the messianic hope represents for an entire people. Once he gets that, he can say at last, "I know now what life was for!"

# VII

## PORTRAIT OF WICKEDNESS

SAMUEL: Mark, we spoke last time of the ideas of judgment and justice, and of goodness, as the Psalmist, or psalmists, conceived these qualities.

VAN DOREN: Yes, particularly under the head of the Law: what it means for a good man to love the Law, how good and how sweet the Law seemed to him.

SAMUEL: Yes, the Law being all-embracing, the Law being, as it were, the symphony of life—and the good man wanted to listen to it. Standing in terrible juxtaposition to that group of ideas, there's the concept of wickedness which recurs again and again as the accompanying motif, in the background: what is the wicked man, what is the essence of wickedness, why are men wicked, and how do we recognize wickedness? This is one of the most important aspects of the psalmodic literature. Psalm 10 gives us a lead to the deeper examination of wickedness in man.

VAN DOREN: Part of that psalm describes a specific man who is wicked. He may not, to be sure, be an individual after all: he may be a *type* of the wicked man. But he's represented in the singular, and he has always interested me a great deal. It might be worth pointing out that the wicked man here is not necessarily wicked *to* the Psalmist. On another occasion, we may speak of the personal adversaries that the Psalmist feels he has—those who are against him. But this now is a description of the man who is wicked, period. I've always remembered Henry David Thoreau saying that most people, when they say a man is good, mean that he is good to *them*.[36] And the contrary could be: most men, when they say that a man is bad, mean that he is bad to *them*.

SAMUEL: That is why, when we recall that we've done somebody a favor, we expect him to do the favor to us, instead of recognizing that if we've done him a favor, then he meets his obligation by doing a favor to anyone at all, not just to us. The favor has to go into circulation.

VAN DOREN: That's right! Here is a portrait, rather an extended portrait, of the wicked man as I think the Psalmist on the whole and generally conceives him:

*His mouth is full of cursing and deceit and oppression;*
*Under his tongue is mischief and iniquity.*
*He sitteth in the lurking-places of the villages;*
*In secret places doth he slay the innocent;*
*His eyes are on the watch for the helpless.*
*He lieth in wait in a secret place as a lion in his lair,*
*He lieth in wait to catch the poor;*
*He doth catch the poor, when he draweth him up in his net.*
*He croucheth, he boweth down,*
*And the helpless fall into his mighty claws.*
*He hath said in his heart: "God hath forgotten;*
*He hideth His face; He will never see."*

*Arise, O Lord; O God, lift up Thy hand;*
*Forget not the humble.*
*Wherefore doth the wicked contemn God,*
*And say in his heart: "Thou wilt not require"?*
*Thou hast seen; for Thou beholdest trouble and vexation, to*
*    requite them with Thy hand;*
*Unto Thee the helpless committeth himself;*
*Thou hast been the helper of the fatherless.*

*Break Thou the arm of the wicked;*
*And as for the evil man, search out his wickedness, till none*
*    be found.*
*The Lord is King for ever and ever;*
*The nations are perished out of His land.*

*Lord, Thou hast heard the desire of the humble:*
*Thou wilt direct their heart, Thou wilt cause Thine ear to*
*    attend;*
*To right the fatherless and the oppressed,*
*That man who is of the earth may be terrible no more.*

SAMUEL: That's a tremendous closing sentence, isn't it?

VAN DOREN: That last line is terrific: "That man who is of the earth may be terrible no more."

SAMUEL: That this humble thing should play the great power—this "hair-crowned bubble of dust," this "forked radish," this "two-legged animal without feathers"![37]

VAN DOREN: That is to say, the man who is purely of earth, who has nothing of God in him.

SAMUEL: You know, in this psalm, almost every aspect of the evil impulse in man is touched on. It's particularly interesting to me that right at the beginning (and we'll meet it in other psalms), there was a terrible dread of a man's tongue. What a man said, the slander which he indulged in, the scurrilities, the spreading of rumors and of evil reports about people —this seems to have occupied the mind of the Psalmist as much as the other aspects, namely, physical domination, oppression, expropriation, exploitation. "His mouth is full of cursing and deceit and oppression"— the *mouth* is full of oppression! You can *kill* a man, of course, just by talking about him. Proverbs has an extraordinary verse: "Death and life are in the power of the tongue; . . ." It isn't just hitting someone, or robbing him, or even killing him physically! PROV. 18:21

VAN DOREN: No one would deny that the man who "lieth in wait to catch the poor," who crouches and waits for the helpless to "fall into his mighty claws," and who even kills his victim—no one would doubt that that man is evil. But apparently, just as evil is the man whose "mouth is full of cursing and deceit and oppression; under his tongue is mischief and iniquity." You're quite right that the evil tongue has a force equal to such things as oppression and exploitation. What's that children's rhyme we hear so often, "Sticks and stones can break my bones, but names will never hurt me."

SAMUEL:   It's not true.

VAN DOREN:   It's not true at all. Only children would say that.

SAMUEL:   As a matter of fact, children are very cruel that way. They suffer a great deal from the name-calling, and this rhyme is a sort of incantation they have, denying what they actually feel. But what my mind turns to at this moment is the verse: "He hath said in his heart: 'God hath forgotten; He hideth His face; He will never see.' " That is to say, the man is detached from the moral principle that is God. He thinks to himself, "All that is pure imagination. I am free to do exactly what I like!" What interests me here is the question of whether such a man—since there is no God for him, no Mover of the universe—doesn't feel necessarily that *he* is God. Since something has to be worshiped, he worships himself. And it occurred to me: such men are always seekers after power. Nowadays we recognize it. The phrase of Lord Acton's, "Power tends to corrupt," has become almost a proverb, hasn't it?

VAN DOREN:   Yes, "and absolute power corrupts absolutely."

SAMUEL:   There's a great depth in that, and as I say, it's become almost like a folkloristic saying. But thinking on this, what engaged my attention was this question: Power in the sense that Lord Acton was using it means power over *people,* doesn't it?

VAN DOREN:   Oh, surely!

SAMUEL:   The question I've asked myself is this: Gaining power over nature, getting the feeling that you are in a sense omnipotent over nature—does that corrupt, too?

VAN DOREN:   I'm sure it does. It has corrupted us already!

SAMUEL:   That's the feeling that, sometimes, moderns get: "We will go to the moon. We will conquer space. If this earth has to fall into the sun and perish, we will find new galaxies to which we will transfer ourselves!" An omnipotence over the entire universe fills people with a pride, and yes, I would say an insolence.

VAN DOREN:   I would say that that was true right here on earth. We have long since ceased to respect the other animals, as I think the authors of the Bible did. We think we're the only one of God's creatures; we think that God created the world for us alone. Whereas all through the Bible, it is so clear to me that we are one of many creations. But we have ceased to believe that. We don't mind what animals we exterminate. We think we have a right to behave just as we please; and that we can move the earth, too. We have machines called "earth movers"! We change the face of the earth.

SAMUEL: "Earth movers!" It's a bit of an exaggeration, although we may ultimately move the earth into smithereens! But we haven't done that yet.

VAN DOREN: No—not yet!

SAMUEL: Dr. Albert Schweitzer summarized this thing we're talking about in his famous phrase, "Reverence for life." The writers of the Bible felt reverence for life in *every* form. I've often thought that the old sacrifices, although they were cruelty to animals, were reverential gestures. Very probably, the eating of meat in early society (as it is today in many of the poorest parts of the world) was a rare occasion; and if one killed an animal in order to eat it, there was a sacrificial element about it. Perhaps there was an unconscious cry of "Forgive me for doing this!" Perhaps it was an acknowledgment of the solemnity of the occasion. But nowadays, the taking of life of animals —particularly the *pointless* extermination of animals— is part of this decline you spoke of just now, this decline in the feeling for the significance of life, which is the basis of the wicked attitude.

VAN DOREN: Yes, and the pointlessness consists in perhaps the very forgetting that the Psalmist here accuses the wicked of: the very forgetting that God exists, that God has His own purposes. The wicked man "hath said in his heart: 'God hath forgotten; He hideth His face; He will never see.' " Incidentally, the wicked man does not deny the existence of God. It's as if he said, "Well, God may exist, as they say, but He doesn't seem to exert Himself anymore. He hasn't spoken, so we are free."

SAMUEL:   The wicked man takes it both ways, as the Epicureans did: "If there are gods, then they don't care what we do. They're indifferent to human needs and suffering."

But let me go back to what I brought up before, Mark: the tongue. Psalm 12 is very powerful on this theme:

> *Help, Lord, for the godly man ceaseth;*
> *For the faithful fail from among the children of men.*
> *They speak falsehood every one with his neighbour;*
> *With flattering lip, and with a double heart, do they speak.*

PSALM
12:2–3

There's that "double heart" we mentioned in our second talk. The Hebrew is *be-lev va-lev*, literally, "with a heart and a heart." In English, we'd say "two-faced." Then the psalm goes on:

> *May the Lord cut off all flattering lips,*
> *The tongue that speaketh proud things!*
> *Who have said: "Our tongue will we make mighty:*
> *Our lips are with us: who is lord over us?"*

PSALM
12:4–5

You know, Mark, the power of the word in the ancient world was certainly as sharply recognized as it is today. We are very fond nowadays of speaking of "the power of the word," both in the affirmative and in the sometimes negative sense. We talk of the abuse of advertising; or the power of the good written word. It's as though our mastery of the means of communications, our power of spreading the word, had made us, for the first time, conscious of the power of the word. But it's not so. Here the Psalmist quotes the arrogant and contemptuous wicked man:

> *May the Lord cut off all flattering lips, . . .*
> *Who have said: "Our tongue will we make mighty; . . ."*

and then the Psalmist cries out the Lord's reply:

PSALM 12:6
> *"For the oppression of the poor, for the sighing of the needy,*
> *Now will I arise," saith the Lord;*
> *"I will set him in safety at whom they puff."*

The Psalmist here is protesting the indignity, the uncleanness with which people are treated in language. This way of speaking is the debasement of the poor; it's not simply that they are physically deprived, but that they are also despised. They are *things* about which one talks contemptuously, looking down on them. This is as important to human beings as physical nourishment.

VAN DOREN: Your word "debasement" points up the meaning of the next verse, Maurice:

PSALM 12:7
> *The words of the Lord are pure words,*
> *As silver tried in a crucible on the earth, refined seven times.*

There's been a debasement of the coinage, and that debasement is evident from the words that men speak when they believe that "God hath forgotten." It doesn't make any difference what anyone says, just as long as he talks loud and long! The words that men say are debased.

SAMUEL: The Hebrew Bible as a whole is very conscious, Mark, of the importance of words, and

of their usage. Some people have said that the Third
Commandment, "Thou shalt not take the name of the
Lord thy God in vain," is perhaps the most important
in the Decalogue, because swearing falsely by the
name of the Lord, or using language to deceive, is the
beginning, and in a certain sense, it is also the conden-
sation of all of the criminal attitudes toward human
beings.[38] All crime in some sense will denote a deception. And the moment you begin to use the name of
the Lord in vain, for an oath which is false and which
you *know* to be false, you are blaspheming. This has
a broader extension: it means also to have a false attitude. Over and over again in the Book of Psalms, we
find this false attitude deplored.

EXOD. 20:7

VAN DOREN:   We passed far too quickly over
a critical phrase in Psalm 12, Maurice: "The godly
man ceaseth," in verse 2. You know, there is almost
a pessimism here and there in the psalms, which says
that there are no good men anymore. "The godly man
ceaseth"—he is a type that has disappeared from the
world. Psalm 14 dwells on that theme and gives a
really terrible indictment of the times:

*The fool hath said in his heart: "There is no God";*
*They have dealt corruptly, they have done abominably;*
*There is none that doeth good.*
*The Lord looked forth from heaven upon the children of men,*
*To see if there were any man of understanding, that did seek*
*    after God.*
*They are all corrupt, they are together become impure;*
*There is none that doeth good, no, not one.*

PSALM
14:1–3

That's a very terrible indictment!

SAMUEL: Yes, it links up with what we shall have to talk about, however briefly, later on, Mark: the psalms of despair. There are times when the Psalmist seems to be throwing up his hands and saying, "It's hopeless! The human being is completely eaten up with vanity, and with wickedness, and it's no use going on!" That recurs again and again, and one of the worst things that the wicked man does—and this is reflected in the psalms—is that he takes away the self-confidence and the assurance of the decent man, who from time to time looks around and says, "What's the use?" There are times when he's overcome by the futility of trying to make headway against this gigantic tide of wickedness, as it seems to him; and of course, that's a *wrong* attitude. We get that kind of cry in the prophet Jeremiah: "Wherefore doth the way of the wicked prosper?" The wicked don't prosper any more than the good: a man who is able could do just as well by being good; but it's his wickedness that *seems* to be the instrument of his success, whereas I don't think that is the case. I don't know how you feel about that, Mark. One of the attitudes in the Book of Psalms is that the wicked man almost invariably falls into a pit.

JER. 12:1

VAN DOREN: Yes, he himself digged the pit for us, but *he* falls into it.

*e.g.*, PSALM
7:16

SAMUEL: Yes, so that when we talk about "Crime doesn't pay," or "Wickedness doesn't pay," we use those words in a very shallow sense. What seems to be indicated in the psalms is that the wicked man—to use an English colloquialism—is "doing himself in"; because actually, if he applied the same persistence, energy, and ingenuity, he could do better in the ordinary sense. And then, the ultimate reality is that a man who does these things is in some sense injuring himself. He doesn't perceive it, but he's injuring himself.

VAN DOREN:   He would seem to be injuring others more than himself, but he's injuring himself most. Maurice, there's one further point I wanted to go on to in this talk, and that is a consideration of this question: whether the Psalmist (and I use that word in the singular, as if one person were saying all these things; it's convenient and practical to do so) ever might be considered guilty of congratulating himself upon his own difference from the wicked. In other words, is he congratulating himself upon his own righteousness; is he censorious in a degree that might make us want to censure *him?* Now I'm not saying this is the case, but I've heard people say something like this. Certainly he is very, very angry at the wicked. You remember how he wants God to punish them— Psalm 58 is a very powerful curse:

*Break their teeth, O God, in their mouth;*                    PSALM
*Break out the cheek-teeth of the young lions, O Lord.*        58:7–12
*Let them melt away as water that runneth apace:*
*When he aimeth his arrows, let them be as though they were*
    *cut off.*
*Let them be as a snail which melteth and passeth away;*
*Like the untimely births of a woman, that have not seen the*
    *sun.*
*Before your pots can feel the thorns,*
*He will sweep it away with a whirlwind, the raw and the*
    *burning alike.*

*The righteous shall rejoice when he seeth the vengeance;*
*He shall wash his feet in the blood of the wicked.*
*And men shall say: "Verily there is a reward for the righ-*
*teous;*
*Verily there is a God that judgeth in the earth."*

And later on, in Psalm 139, again speaking of the
wicked, the Psalmist says:

PSALM          *I hate them with utmost hatred;*
139:22         *I count them mine enemies.*

Those are wonderful and very powerful statements.

SAMUEL:   Let me make a little digression. I
love that phrase: "Before your pots can feel the
thorns." It's a lovely figure. In the desert, they gather
thorns and light them under the pot. That was one of
the forms of fuel, and it's a very charming and striking
figure.

But now, adverting to this subject you've
raised: there is no question in my mind that there are
passages in the psalms in which the speaker places
himself in the category of the self-righteous. I've always had an uneasy feeling about Psalm 37, a passage
of which is recited daily in the Grace after meals in
full. The passage goes:

PSALM          *I have been young, and now am old;*
37:25          *Yet have I not seen the righteous forsaken,*
               *Nor his seed begging bread.*

When a pious Jewish family has a stranger at table—
some poor man—that portion is always said in a low
voice, so as not to shame the guest who might be there
because he hasn't got anywhere else to go for a meal.

I'm uneasy about that. Even though I told you earlier that I don't believe in cutting out *anything at all* from the Bible, that passage gives me pause, especially now after the Hitler calamity. I feel a touch of self-righteousness in it. You can almost imagine the Psalmist saying, "Look, I'm all right; I'm eating, and that's because I have been just."

VAN DOREN:    I may surprise you now, Maurice, by saying I'm not sure that this is true. It seems to me that there *is* a real place for indignation against wickedness. I think we have too little of it these days. I'm appalled sometimes how calmly a great many people take the fact that the world is full of wickedness now. It is, of course; always has been. And I hope I'm not being censorious, or I hope I'm not putting on the robes of judgment when I say so. But you yourself spoke of an almost unparalleled period of wickedness half a generation ago, didn't you, when you mentioned Hitler?

SAMUEL:    Yes, this was the reference.

VAN DOREN:    And I am very much interested to remember at this moment a little story told by C. S. Lewis in his book on the psalms,[39] which both of us read while we were thinking about this subject. Lewis tells how he was on a train in England one night early in the Second World War, and he overheard some young British soldiers talking to one another about how their own government had probably just used propaganda to get them into the war. They simply took it for granted that their own government was

saying things about the Nazis which were probably
lies, in order to whip up the kind of enthusiasm that
would "pep up" the troops and lead to enlistment.
Mister Lewis remarked that this made him unhappy
and even bitter on two counts: one was that they
hadn't believed the things that were true about the
Nazis; but, he said, maybe worse than that was the fact
that here were these young men quite calmly saying,
"Our government has deceived us," as if that were a
matter of course, an everyday occurrence! And it
didn't seem to bother them!

SAMUEL:    That brings me back to another element in the psalms—the question of the lie as the first
foundation of evil-doing.

VAN DOREN:    Which is what Dante, by the
way, based the whole of his moral system on in *The
Divine Comedy.*

SAMUEL:    Psalm 34 has a brief passage that
is included in the daily prayers of the Jews, closing
the most important of the prayers. The passage
goes:

PSALM          *Keep thy tongue from evil,*
34:14          *And thy lips from speaking guile.*

In the daily prayer, the "thy" becomes "my." The
man asks to be helped not to practice deception on
people; he prays not to be misled into misstatement
and into the deception of other human beings. And

once a man feels that he is not lying, he feels safer about not committing the other crimes and misdemeanors against his fellow mortals.

VAN DOREN: I'm glad that we took this opportunity to speak of something so dark and bitter in the psalms, Maurice. I dare say there are many people who shared my illusion some time ago that the psalms were lighter in quality pervasively than they are. But they have their darkness, too, and I think it's very important to continue probing into the dark side in our next talk.

# VIII

## ENTER THE ADVERSARY

SAMUEL: Mark, something is left over in my
mind from our last talk. I was thinking of your observation that there is a lack of moral indignation in the
modern world in contrast with perhaps an excess, as I
intimated—at any rate, certainly, a plenitude—of
moral indignation in the Book of Psalms and elsewhere in the Hebrew Bible. I gave a lot of thought
particularly to the justification for your remark about
the absence today of moral indignation. It seems to me
that there are several points of view from which we
can see this feeling of moral dismay being eaten at,
corroded, so that it ceases to play a part in contemporary life. (When I speak of "moral dismay," I am
thinking of it as apart from mere social disapproval.)

We talk nowadays of someone being what he

is—a bad person, a slanderer, a liar, an oppressor, a show-off, or whatever—as the result of the social system. "Society" made him what he is; "society" is therefore guilty. One might say that the person in question has had nothing to do with it. That's one point of view. From another point of view, people say of this person, "What happened was that he was frightened by a big yellow dog when he was a baby, and ever since then, this is the way in which he responds to that memory, whether it is conscious with him, or whether it is unconscious." All sorts of no doubt valid observations of that kind are used as an excuse for complete moral—one might say—indifference. Certainly I cannot agree with those people who say, "X is not a responsible person; what he needs is a cure and not a course in moral sensitivity." I would suggest not a cure, but the awakening of his moral perceptiveness.

VAN DOREN:   There are those who explain any iniquity in an individual by saying that it was "caused" by society; there are "social reasons" for it —as if there were nothing but society!

SAMUEL:   Yes! Individuals have no responsibility—only society. Individuals don't exist—only society.

VAN DOREN:   And also—as the Psalmist would say—as if there were not a God above or beyond society. Society is nothing but the men that exist, is that not true?

SAMUEL:   Yes.

VAN DOREN:   And the Psalmist is quite right in saying that many of those men, if not most of them, are somehow sadly imperfect. To assume that society is anything more than just the aggregation of individuals (I happen to think that's all society is: it's just all the people that there are); that it has some kind of validity; that it's even a kind of god rather than a sheer aggregation, is to forget what this book is constantly trying to remind us of. This book, the Bible, is continuously teaching us that outside of nature (and nature includes created beings), there is a force, an intellect, an understanding—

SAMUEL:   To which the individual is related.

VAN DOREN:   Yes! And his deepest and most personal relation is to *that,* rather than to society, or nature, or history, or the times, or any other abstraction.

SAMUEL:   Of course, apart from the points of view I've already mentioned, we often hear the purely deterministic attitude expressed, which says: "What I do isn't me, isn't merely society; this is the dance of the atoms. And therefore, let's have no moral judgment at all." And I see more and more clearly, you're perfectly right in demanding that there should be a moral attitude of condemnation or of approval. The fact that it's difficult to draw the line—not to overdo it—doesn't plead against it. One must neither underdo it nor overdo it; there must be a proper and balanced attitude on these questions.

VAN DOREN: My point, Maurice, merely was: if this element had been lacking in the Book of Psalms, something very important would have been left out.

SAMUEL: There couldn't have been any psalms without it; there couldn't have been a Bible if there wasn't the moral responsibility of the individual!

VAN DOREN: That word "adversary" came up in our last talk, Maurice, and I'd like to consider it more closely. The word appears very frequently in the Book of Psalms. I never used to know how common it was until I reread the book and the frequency struck me. David himself, speaking in Psalm 3 at a time, supposedly, when he is fleeing from the rebellion led *see* II SAM. by his son, Absalom, says: 15ff.

> *Lord, how many are mine adversaries become!*    PSALM
> *Many are they that rise up against me.*    3:2–4
> *Many there are that say of my soul:*
> *"There is no salvation for him in God."*
>
> *But Thou, O Lord, art a shield about me;*
> *My glory, and the lifter up of my head.*

He continues on to say that God will defend and protect him against those who say such things about him. Nevertheless, there is the statement that he has many, many adversaries, and that theme runs through the entire Book of Psalms. It's not present in every psalm, of course, but it appears often enough so that I think we would be culpable if we neglected it.

SAMUEL: Oh, we can't neglect that. One of the reasons that we can defend the notion of David as having been one of the chief writers of the psalms is precisely because of the kind of life he had: the continuous, particularly intimate struggles he engaged in would leave him with a permanent impression of hostilities or possible hostilities around him. (I say "intimate," thinking of his struggle with Saul, his father-in-law, and with Absalom, his beloved son.)

VAN DOREN: You know, everyone in a position of eminence or authority is of course surrounded by such persons. I'm told that you cannot exaggerate what it means to be President of the United States, in terms of the hostility and the ill-will that pour upon you from all directions.

SAMUEL: Tennyson said it in *Idylls of the King:* it's "that fierce light which beats upon a throne."

VAN DOREN: I've never forgotten, for instance, talking once with Richard Cleveland, the son of Grover Cleveland, who told me something of what his mother had endured. She was a young and very beautiful woman who married Grover Cleveland when he was President of the United States. She had had no experience at all in being in the public limelight, and the son said that she was never, never able to understand the virulence of the abuse that was poured upon her husband, sometimes for reasons that, to be sure, were intelligible; but in many cases, for reasons that were not intelligible—just pure hatred, pure animosity, pure jealousy, envy, perhaps, of distinction. I believe that happens to every president, prime minister, or king.

SAMUEL: Well, if you're in a prominent position, it means that you're talked about. And inevitably, if you're talked about, it will be in a friendly or in a hostile fashion. Certainly it could be David who complained:

> *Unrighteous witnesses rise up;*
> *They ask me of things that I know not.*

PSALM
35:11

It makes one think that somebody probably wanted a Grover Cleveland to change the weather, and when he couldn't, then went around complaining, "Well, what have we got a president for?" There pours in upon the man in top position a constant stream; the people abreact on him their feeling of frustration: "There's the strong man; why doesn't he do something about it?"—as though he were omnipotent! And then David goes on to complain about these people:

> *They repay me evil for good;*
> *Bereavement is come to my soul.*
> *But as for me, when they were sick, my clothing was sackcloth,*
> *I afflicted my soul with fasting;*
> *And my prayer, may it return into mine own bosom.*

PSALM
35:12–13

That last line means, "The things that I wished for *them,* let those things happen to *me.* I would be content!"

VAN DOREN: It's a very moving and really quite terrible thing David is saying. Apparently David had once been very close to these people who are now his adversaries (or adversary; David uses the singular at one point):

*I went about as though it had been my friend or my brother;*
*I bowed down mournful, as one that mourneth for his mother.*

That is to say, when the adversary experienced ill times.

*But when I halt they rejoice, and gather themselves together;*
*The abjects gather themselves together against me, and those*
*  whom I know not;*
*They tear me, and cease not;*
*With the profanest mockeries of backbiting*
*They gnash at me with their teeth.*

SAMUEL:    David can't stand the evil talk. That seems to eat him up as much as anything else!

VAN DOREN:    This is a very graphic description of what would appear to be pure, unmotivated ill will. Later on in that psalm, his enemies "rejoice" over him; they "wink with the eye" at him, and they hate him "without a cause." He goes on to say:

*For they speak not peace;*
*But they devise deceitful matters against them that are quiet*
*  in the land.*
*Yea, they open their mouth wide against me;*
*They say: "Aha, aha, our eye hath seen it."*

Seen *what?* The implication is that there had been nothing to see, but they claim that there was.

SAMUEL:    What is it that cuts so deeply into us and rankles when people speak bad things behind our backs? There seems to be a special torment attached to the consciousness of bad rumors or bad interpretations of our actions going among people.

VAN DOREN: Of course, the law recognizes that statements of *truth* about us can be just as damaging as statements of untruth.

SAMUEL: Yes! I suppose we always carry around with us an image of what we are like in the minds of people—and we are very tender about that image. We like to imagine that we are well thought of, and that we have status; and every evidence to the contrary, that people are willing to listen to evil statements about us shocks us. We say, "It isn't like that at all!" One of my tests for being an adult would be this: to be able to take both like and dislike of yourself from other people, and to know that neither of them is deserved. For me, this is the sign of being grown-up —you don't yield your personality, but you recognize that people can't know you anyhow.

VAN DOREN: Oh, that's perfectly true—although adulthood, as you're describing it now, is a very exalted state. There are very few people who can arrive at the position where they *really* don't care what people think of them. It's almost unheard of, isn't it?

SAMUEL: I would paraphrase Psalm 37 and say: "I have been young, and now I am old, and I don't know what it is to be an adult." *(laughing)* I *still* don't feel grown-up.

VAN DOREN:    David, at any rate, carries right
to the very end this lamentation of his, Maurice, concerning those who backbite. And I might raise a question that is similar to the one I raised in our last talk:
whether he ever becomes excessive in this. I'm not
saying that he does; I'm only saying that his statement
always, if anything, is the full statement, the extreme
statement, as it is here. I'm personally glad that it is
extreme, because it becomes classic. In Psalm 55 he
says, for example:

PSALM        *And I said: "Oh that I had wings like a dove!*
55:7–9       *Then would I fly away, and be at rest.*
             *Lo, then would I wander far off,*
             *I would lodge in the wilderness.*
             *I would haste me to a shelter*
             *From the stormy wind and tempest."*

He feels this slander so acutely that he wants to get out
of the world altogether. The only refuge from it is to
cease to be in the world.

SAMUEL:    There's a very moving phrase in
Yiddish: *Mentshn zol mir nit hobn in zeyere mayler* ("People shouldn't have me in their mouths"). People
shouldn't talk about me. Forget about me, rather than
have this derogation of my dignity!

VAN DOREN:    David then goes on to implore
the Lord to protect him by destroying his enemies, or
their lies:

PSALM        *Destroy, O Lord, and divide their tongue;*
55:10–12     *For I have seen violence and strife in the city.*
             *Day and night they go about it upon the walls thereof;*

*Iniquity also and mischief are in the midst of it.*
*Wickedness is in the midst thereof;*
*Oppression and guile depart not from her broad place.*

SAMUEL: The Psalmist—whether it was David or someone else—had had what we call nowadays a traumatic experience: a beloved one had betrayed him.

VAN DOREN: Goodness has been repaid with evil. He says:

*For it was not an enemy that taunted me,*       PSALM
*Then I could have borne it; . . .*               55:13

SAMUEL: But of course he could not have borne it. He's just adding this now as a sort of extra bonus to his sentiments!

VAN DOREN: Here's the whole bitter passage about his betrayer:

*For it was not an enemy that taunted me,*       PSALM
*Then I could have borne it;*                     55:13–15
*Neither was it mine adversary that did magnify himself*
    *against me,*
*Then I would have hid myself from him.*
*But it was thou, a man mine equal,*
*My companion, and my familiar friend;*
*We took sweet counsel together,*
*In the house of God we walked with the throng.*

This terrible feeling of betrayal is something that we all can understand. Shakespeare understood it thoroughly. I remember suddenly two moments from his works that have this same intense feeling: when

Othello finds out that Iago, his nearest friend, companion, and adviser, has all the time been his enemy; and when Julius Caesar, surrounded by the conspirators who are stabbing him, suddenly sees his friend Brutus lifting a knife against him, and he asks, "Et tu, Brute?" I can imagine both Othello and Julius Caesar saying, "If this had been mine adversary, I could have borne it, but it was my faithful friend!"

SAMUEL: The foundations simply fall away from under your feet. If such a man becomes your adversary, then you can understand the constant harping of the Psalmist on this man, and his preoccupation with the people who wish him evil, and do him evil. Psalm 109 is a very powerful utterance of what he'd like to see done to this adversary. But let me digress for a moment. We were speaking before, Mark, about how people can't stand being spoken ill of. Do you think, Mark, that this has something to do also with the primitive feeling about the power of the word? If a man curses you, you feel that he is inflicting damage not simply to your reputation, but is setting loose some power against you. Is that your feeling?

VAN DOREN: Yes. Harm is unleashed not merely against your reputation, but against *you*. It's as if you personally were being undermined and corrupted and dissolved. Oh, yes! I'm sure that's true. I've seen a few instances of this in my time: someone suddenly turning against someone else and saying things that—well, we can call them "unforgivable." When we say that, we mean really that it's as if the victim of the curse had been destroyed.

SAMUEL:   X says to Y in a rage, "You be damned!" Now, a tremor of fear goes through Y. Perhaps it's a warning to him that he *deserves* damnation, and an evil power is being reminded that he should be damned.

VAN DOREN:   Maurice, you mentioned Psalm 109. I'm interested in that psalm because it contains a speech made by a slanderous and malicious adversary. It's in quotation marks, and we learn quite specifically now what sort of thing it is that the adversary has said.

SAMUEL:   It puts me in mind of the old story of two Jews coming away from prayer on Yom Kippur, the Day of Atonement, when they've forgiven each other all their sins, and one of them says to the other, "I wish you everything that you wish me." And the other says, "What? Are you starting again!"

Now, this is what that adversary has in mind. The adversary is praying to God, and saying[40] what should happen to—let's say to David, if David is the Psalmist:

> "Set Thou a wicked man over him;
> And let an adversary stand at his right hand.
> When he is judged, let him go forth condemned;
> And let his prayer be turned into sin.
> Let his days be few;
> Let another take his charge."

PSALM
109:6–8

By the way, from the length of the curse, we can see that the speaker really didn't want the Psalmist's days to be few, because he had to have a long life to be the recipient of all these benefactions!

*"Let his children be fatherless,*
*And his wife a widow.*
*Let his children be vagabonds, and beg;*
*And let them seek their bread out of their desolate places."*

That's a ghastly thought!

*"Let the creditor distrain all that he hath;*
*And let strangers make spoil of his labor.*
*Let there be none to extend kindness unto him;*
*Neither let there be any to be gracious unto his fatherless*
*children.*
*Let his posterity be cut off;*
*In the generation following let their name be blotted out.*
*Let the iniquity of his fathers be brought to remembrance unto*
*the Lord;*
*And let not the sin of his mother be blotted out.*
*Let them be before the Lord continually,*
*That He may cut off the memory of them from the earth.*
*Because that he remembered not to do kindness,*
*But persecuted the poor and needy man,*
*And the broken in heart he was ready to slay. . . ."*

Now this is David, or the Psalmist, complaining:
"That's my adversary! That's the kind of thing he says
about me!" Just to read it makes your blood run cold!
You know, Mark, there are many people who actually
read those little printed cards from machines that tell
your character or forecast your future, and when they
read them, something happens! They know it's nonsense, yet something reacts inside when they read the
words: "You are a very able and brilliant person"; or
"You've done foolish things." The power of the word
is not to be overcome so easily.

VAN DOREN:   Even though it's just a little,
miserable slip of pasteboard that cost a penny to get

out of a machine, yes. But there is superstition in all of us, I suppose, at this point; we can't help thinking that maybe the moment was chosen when those particular words should be conveyed to us. This speech put in the mouth of an adversary is perfectly dreadful.

SAMUEL:   Mark, you asked last time about a certain element of self-righteousness in the psalms.

VAN DOREN:   And I asked whether that element was here, too.

SAMUEL:   Let's consider a verse like this:

*They that hate me without a cause are more than the hairs*     PSALM 69:5
*of my head;*
*They that would cut me off, being mine enemies wrongfully,*
*are many; . . .*

Well now, there is *no* man that is hated at *every* point without cause. If there is such a thing as justifiable hate (we'll not debate that!), then certainly every man has given cause for being hated. If this is King David, surely the relatives of Uriah the Hittite, let us say, had every reason to hate him; surely the relatives of Saul; possibly even the relatives of Nabal, the husband of Abigail. So that I would put this statement under the heading of "unjustified self-righteousness." The man doesn't ask himself, "What have I done?" Instead he says, "I've always been good to everybody, and look, they repay me always with evil!" Whenever I hear a person speak that way, I'm quite certain that he has enemies.

VAN DOREN:    Of course, there's the thing frequently said about the psalms, that they speak for everybody; that they're not to be understood purely in
terms of individual utterance. And in that case, these
psalms might have the value of being expressions of an
experience that all people have, namely, of learning
that they are spoken ill of. Therefore this psalm could
be taken not only unto himself by any individual who's
reading it, but even could be thought of as having
collective significance. Any of us—meaning *all* of us—
are so spoken of.

SAMUEL:    Mark, I don't think we have paid
enough attention to what we mentioned at the beginning, and that is the psalms not as individual utterances, but as a folk utterance—having an application
to the state of a people, as well as to the claims and
clamors of an individual. Any people in the world—
the Jewish people, any ancient people, any modern
people, let us say, the Americans, the British, the Sovi-
ets—that says, "I am hated without a cause," has no
more right to say it than any other people, and no
more right to say it than any other individual. Not that
the hatred is justified or not—though the hatred might
not be excessive; and not that there isn't hatred without a cause. But to think of oneself as being guiltless,
of not *ever* having precipitated the hostility of a single
human being, is a form of self-righteousness.

# IX

# MUSIC OF DESPAIR

SAMUEL: Mark, we ventured into the dark
side of the psalms last time when we considered some
of the utterances of the Psalmist concerning his feelings toward the wicked. He is sometimes overwhelmed by their ubiquity and persistence, and passages in the psalms express his horror and even his
passionate hatred of evil and of evildoers. But the
cumulative effect of his intense emotion could, and
often did, culminate in downright despair, so that in
the psalms we now find a body of material which re-
lates to despair as such: a man's feeling of being—as
we say nowadays—"down and out." Yet, the feeling
of despair is so powerfully stated that when a man is
in that mood, I think it's a relief for him to discover

how perfectly it has been uttered for him; and he finds a kind of refuge in the fact that it *has* been felt, it *has* been expressed—and men have survived it! Some people have said that such utterances should *not* appear in the sacred writings because they discourage rather than lift. Do you feel that is the case at all?

VAN DOREN: I'm afraid that is not a real question, Maurice. You know what my answer would be, don't you?

SAMUEL: Yes, but I want *others* to know it!

VAN DOREN *(laughing):* My answer is certainly that this book would not be the great book it is —the supreme book it is—if it left anything out of the human score. This is music of despair, music out of the very depths—and, as a matter of fact, that is a phrase which is used here: "out of the very depths." That's been translated *de profundis* in Latin. If the depths were not spoken *out of* here, neither could the heights be spoken *from.* The heights and the depths have to talk to one another, and they do in this book, which covers the entire field of feeling and of experience, it seems to me. No, far from wishing this unsaid, I'm very happy that it *was* said, terrible as the cries are. I think immediately of the verses that open Psalm 22:

PSALM
22:2–4

*My God, my God, why hast Thou forsaken me,*
*And art far from my help at the words of my cry?*
*O my God, I call by day, but Thou answerest not;*
*And at night, and there is no surcease for me.*
*Yet Thou art holy,*
*O Thou that art enthroned upon the praises of Israel.*

And he goes on once more to enumerate the evil that
is done to him, saying finally:

> *Be not far from me; for trouble is near;*          PSALM
> *For there is none to help.*                        22:12–15
> *Many bulls have encompassed me;*
> *Strong bulls of Bashan have beset me round.*
> *They open wide their mouth against me,*
> *As a ravening and a roaring lion.*
> *I am poured out like water,*
> *And all my bones are out of joint;*
> *My heart is become like wax;*
> *It is melted in mine inmost parts.*

You notice how physical the images are. His very
body is destroyed, as well as his peace of mind.

SAMUEL:   He seems to be thinking, as it were,
with his body. He's giving utterance with his actual
physical being to his emotions.

VAN DOREN:   This is a mood that is, of
course, not confined to this great book. I suddenly remember a poem of Thomas Hardy called *God-
forgotten,* in which he talks about a whole world which
God seems to have forgotten, but it is a terrible thing
for him to think about. The feeling that we have been
forgotten by God is of course very different from that
of the wicked man, about whom we spoke last time,
the wicked man who said: "God is not noticing any
more. God has forgotten us. We don't need to worry
about Him any more."

SAMUEL:   Isn't it a pity that a powerful, almost
crushing phrase like "God-forsaken" has become

slangy! People talk of "Oh, that God-forsaken place,
that God-forsaken house"—whereas it's one of the
most terrible phrases that one can conjure up!

VAN DOREN: Or "This God-forsaken fountain pen!" It could be anything.

SAMUEL: My eye fastened on a verse in Psalm
22 which you omitted, Mark:

PSALM
22:4–5

*Yet Thou art holy,*
*O Thou that art enthroned upon the praises of Israel.*
*In Thee did our fathers trust;*
*They trusted, and Thou didst deliver them.*

Notice, again it is the individual mingling with the
people, so that the utterance can be for the person, and
it can be for the community which—we've observed
more than once—is a characteristic of the Jewish outlook from of old. The man and the organism called
"the Jewish people" mingle and intermingle, separate,
and come together again. But I was going to remark:
about the despair expressed by the Psalmist, you always get the sensation that he's touching bottom, and
there's no alternative except to reverse his course.
That is perhaps the psychological effect. A story is told
about a Hasidic rabbi who had gone through a series
of misfortunes, Job-like. His family had been wiped
out, his means of sustenance had been taken away
from him, and suddenly he began to laugh. The people around him asked, "But why are you laughing?"
And he replied, "There's nowhere to go now but up!"
That's the sensation you sometimes get from reading
these psalms; and that's their therapeutic effect.

VAN DOREN:   It's uncanny, Maurice, how you keep reminding me—with or without intending to do so—of things that are here. Surely the Psalmist, when he says that he is in the nethermost pit (he has been thrown down into a pit and is indeed at the very bottom of it), is talking about the idea you mentioned. The bottom of the pit would be a place no deeper than which you can go, of course.

*see* PSALM<br>88:7

SAMUEL:   That's absolute zero. You can't get below absolute zero. If you're going anywhere, it's into a higher temperature.

VAN DOREN:   I'm terribly interested, Maurice, that at one point in the midst of his lamentations of despair, the Psalmist has a flash of insight. In his anguish, he's never accusing God of having forgotten him; he's only crying out in his fear that this might be so. But in the middle of Psalm 77, suddenly he wonders whether it's a mistake on his part to think so, whether it's just a kind of malady in his own mind:

> *And I say* [as it were, to myself]: *"This is my weakness,*
> *That the right hand of the Most High could change.*
> *I will make mention of the deeds of the Lord;*
> *Yea, I will remember Thy wonders of old. . . ."*

PSALM<br>77:11–12

You see, again I think the book wouldn't be as valuable as it is if it didn't somehow always search for correction of itself. These outcries of despair alternate with feelings that maybe the despair is improper, even blasphemous. And the Psalmist says, "Well, it may be only my weakness that makes me cry out so." And we can suspect that, too.

SAMUEL:   There's one last stand, so to speak,
which he takes when he gets down to this absolute
zero. He thinks of death, and death seems to him to
be an impossible sort of thing. It's almost a blasphemy.
He cries out against it, saying in Psalm 88: "If I'm
dead, that's no good for You. I can't praise You!" He
asks rhetorically:

PSALM          *Wilt Thou work wonders for the dead?*
88:11          *Or shall the shades arise and give Thee thanks?*

Earlier in that same psalm, he's brooded about being
dead:

PSALM          *I am counted with them that go down into the pit;*
88:5–6         *I am become as a man that hath no help;*
               *Set apart among the dead,*
               *Like the slain that lie in the grave,*
               *Whom Thou rememberest no more;*
               *And they are cut off from Thy hand.*

He protests against the fact that once he has been
wiped out, so much is missing in the accounts of the
universe, and there is one voice less to praise and exalt
the Almighty.

VAN DOREN:   That's terribly touching. It's as
if he were saying, "You do not listen to me now. Your
ears seem to be closed to me. Think how impossible
it will be to hear from me when I am dead, when I'm
in the underworld from which no voice ever comes."

SAMUEL:   It reminds me quite tangentially of
a funny remark that Doctor Johnson once made. He
was walking along with Boswell, and turned to him

and said, "You know, Bozzie, it suddenly occurs to me that when I'm in the grave, I shall get no letters." In the grave, there's no receiving and no answering of letters—and Johnson protests against it!

VAN DOREN:   Even though he might have thought that in life, letters were a trouble and a nuisance. You know, we all get too many letters. They pile up on our desk unanswered. Yet we may not like to think of a time when we'd have none at all!

SAMUEL:   Well, they won't accumulate for too long, of course. People would begin to find out, or, receiving no reply, they'd give up. But returning to Psalm 88, Mark, notice that the Psalmist gives a very powerful indication of how he and his contemporaries felt with regard to immortality: they didn't bother about it! The Psalmist expresses the view that the main purpose of life, its justification, is that living, you are in contact with God; dead, you haven't any contact. Being here on earth, being active and praising God is the climactic expression of a man's significance.

VAN DOREN:   The phrase, "out of the depths," to which I referred a minute ago, opens Psalm 130. I'm not sure but what this short psalm sums up the whole of our discussion of the desperate man:

> *Out of the depths have I called Thee, O Lord.*      PSALM 130
> *Lord, hearken unto my voice;*
> *Let Thine ears be attentive*
> *To the voice of my supplications.*

*If Thou, Lord, shouldest mark iniquities,*
*O Lord, who could stand?*
*For with Thee there is forgiveness,*
*That Thou mayest be feared.*

*I wait for the Lord, my soul doth wait,*
*And in His word do I hope.*
*My soul waiteth for the Lord,*
*More than watchmen for the morning;*
*Yea, more than watchmen for the morning.*

*O Israel, hope in the Lord;*
*For with the Lord there is mercy,*
*And with Him is plenteous redemption.*
*And He will redeem Israel*
*From all his iniquities.*

The end of that psalm, incidentally, confirms me in my belief that you're quite right in assuming there is always a collective as well as an individual voice here. Suddenly there's a shift from the first-person singular to the first-person plural, an invocation to all of Israel to hope in the Lord, as the Psalmist is saying that *he* should. But the word "supplications" interests me: "Let Thine ears be attentive/ To the voice of my supplications." In other words, this isn't despair, after all. This is only the most momentary fear, or conviction, that there is no communication.

SAMUEL: It's the last black hour which has in it implicit, as they say, the coming of the dawn. It's the piling up on a man of the immense pyramid of human woe and human hostility, the feeling that God has forsaken him, and the sign of it is that all his enemies have the power to do whatever they like with him. And then—a break. Suddenly, there is a widening. He

is set at large. Robert Browning has a poem which
appositely illustrates exactly what I mean by this sudden quick turn, the transition from despair into the
power of supplication. You know it, Mark; it's the
story of the tyrant who thought he could exterminate
a man. Here is the tyrant speaking:[41]

*Of the million or two, more or less,*
*I rule and possess,*
*One man, for some cause undefined,*
*Was least to my mind.*

*I struck him, he grovelled of course—*
*For, what was his force?*
*I pinned him to earth with my weight*
*And persistence of hate:*
*And he lay, would not moan, would not curse,*
*As his lot might be worse.*

*"Were the object less mean, would he stand*
*At the swing of my hand!*
*For obscurity helps him and blots*
*The hole where he squats." . . .*

*Had he kith now or kin, were access*
*To his heart, did I press: . . .*
*No: I could not but smile through my chafe:*
*For the fellow lay safe*
*As his mates do, the midge and the nit,*
*—Through minuteness, to wit. . . .*

*So, I soberly laid my last plan*
*To extinguish the man.*
*Round his creep-hole, with never a break*
*Ran my fires for his sake;*
*Overhead, did my thunder combine*
*With my underground mine;*
*Till I looked from my labor content*
*To enjoy the event.*

*When sudden . . . how think ye, the end?*
*Did I say, "without friend"?*
*Say rather, from marge to blue marge*
*The whole sky grew his targe*
*With the sun's self for visible boss,*
*While an Arm ran across*
*Which the earth heaved beneath like a breast*
*Where the wretch was safe prest!*
*Do you see? Just my vengeance complete,*
*The man sprang to his feet,*
*Stood erect, caught at God's skirts, and prayed!*
*—So, I was afraid!*

This is Browning at his best, with his insight into human emotions and that great optimism of his. This is the turning point from despair to supplication that you were referring to.

VAN DOREN:  The turning point in Browning's poem, I take it, is in the man, not the great tyrant, isn't it?

SAMUEL:  Yes, the victim experiences the turning point. Browning had this beautiful dramatic power of conveying character through a person's conversation, and also of casting a light upon other persons through that same conversation. The victim of the tyrant suddenly perceives that all he has to do is pray; and in standing up and praying, he defeats the tyrant.

VAN DOREN:  Maurice, it occurs to me to say just now that we are perhaps almost precisely at the middle of our series of conversations about the Book of Psalms. *We* have reached the bottom of our subject, too. We have gone down into the pit of despair, and henceforth, I believe, the movement is entirely up. I see ahead really the most beautiful, the most peaceful, and the most lovely and loving utterances in the whole book.

SAMUEL:   Yes, the psalms in themselves—not merely by the arrangement of our discussion—the psalms in themselves rise to that glorious climax of the last praises which beat like cymbals through all space. There's a reverberation of praise and glory at the end which has left the world astounded ever since they were first given to us.

VAN DOREN:   But those great musical works would not have the force they have, I think, if behind them, or beneath them, were not these bass drums of despair and of bitterness. Do you agree?

SAMUEL:   This is the background.

VAN DOREN:   This is the place from which the psalms now climb.

SAMUEL:   The beating and the throbbing die down. You remember how in Tchaikovsky's *1812 Overture,* gradually the Russian hymn rises over "The Marseillaise." The invader is, as it were, inundated by the cry of hope from the invaded country. So it happens here. And the turning point is, as you've intimated, the movement from despair to supplication.

VAN DOREN:   And of course, Maurice, if the Psalmist had truly despaired, if really in his mind he had concluded there was nothing left for him, he would have become silent. Whereas he keeps on singing. The very fact even that he *tries* to express his despair means that he hasn't given up.

SAMUEL: It means that he is *not* in total despair, because despair in the ultimate sense means that you've given up, and you die. The expression of real despair is death. In this same vein, a man's supreme contempt for the world doesn't lie in uttering brutal epigrams about the world. I've often thought that Diogenes in his tub, showing off to Alexander, saying, "All I want of you is to get out of the sunlight,"[42] was not the cynic he pretended to be, because if he had really been a cynic, he would have paid no attention whatsoever to the mighty ruler who came to visit him. But to the extent that he wanted to put Alexander in his place, he was interested in Alexander, and interested in instructing the world.

VAN DOREN: Right!

SAMUEL: Similarly, you've got to look into the motives of the man who goes about proclaiming the wickedness of people. You ask yourself, "What's he driving at?" There is left in him a belief that *some* goodness exists; were it not for that goodness, he would have no one to appeal to! One doesn't go talking to a wicked world about the wickedness of the world if there isn't something good to hang onto!

VAN DOREN: Exactly! Because one wouldn't assume that the wicked world would be in the slightest degree interested. No, there must be a reference beyond and above, or outside. As a matter of fact, the Psalmist never stops longing for the attention of God. In one of our talks, you yourself referred to that wonderful beginning of Psalm 42:

> *As the hart panteth after the water brooks,*      PSALM 42:2
> *So panteth my soul after Thee, O God.*

The Psalmist has never ceased to feel this longing. Later on in that same psalm, he addresses himself:

> *Why art thou cast down, O my soul?*      PSALM
> *And why moanest thou within me?*      42:12
> *Hope thou in God; for I shall yet praise Him,*
> *The salvation of my countenance, and my God.*

No, the connection is never actually cut. It's merely that the Psalmist has gone as deep as he can go, yet retaining his faith that there is something at least to be lost *from.*

SAMUEL: That note of the physical you were referring to in our earlier talks occurs always in connection with prayer. There's a *thirst* in the man. You mentioned Psalm 42. Psalm 63 uses the same image:

> *My soul thirsteth for Thee, my flesh longeth for Thee,*      PSALM
> *In a dry and weary land, where no water is.*      63:2–7
> *So have I looked for Thee in the sanctuary,*
> *To see Thy power and Thy glory. . . .*
>
> *So will I bless Thee as long as I live;*
> *In Thy name will I lift up my hands.*
>
> *My soul is satisfied as with marrow and fatness;*
> *And my mouth doth praise Thee with joyful lips;*
> *When I remember Thee upon my couch,*
> *And meditate on Thee in the night-watches.*

He is interfused with this feeling of return, lifted up
from despair; suddenly, to use his own figure, it is like
a wave of water passing through him, and drenching
his spirit with what Isaiah once called "water out of the
ISAIAH       wells of salvation."
12:3

VAN DOREN:    I'm sure it's a fact that throughout the whole literature of religious ecstasy expressed
in words, the theme of thirst or drought has been the
classic theme for spiritual failure. In any kind of poet,
in any religion, I suspect, this may turn out to be true.
By contrast, the image of spiritual success is rain, a
fresh spring, waters running and leaping, dew and
wetness generally—and of course, birds singing, too.

SAMUEL:    That would be true especially in
lands where rain is scarce, as it was, and still is, in
Israel, where every drop of water coming down from
the heavens is looked upon as a source of life.

VAN DOREN:    The English poet Gerard Manley Hopkins is particularly powerful on this subject.
He ends one of his sonnets, "O thou lord of life, send
my roots rain."[43]

SAMUEL:    You mentioned birds, Mark. One
of the best-known of all the psalms has a passage that
sings itself. The English is very beautiful:

PSALM        *How lovely are Thy tabernacles, O Lord of hosts!*
84:2-4       *My soul yearneth, yea, even pineth for the courts of the Lord;*
             *My heart and my flesh sing for joy unto the living God.*
             *Yea, the sparrow hath found a house, and the swallow a nest*
             *   for herself,*

*Where she may lay her young;*
*Thine altars, O Lord of hosts,*
*My King, and my God—.*

And a few verses later, Mark, we find one of the most
famous passages in the whole Bible:

*For a day in Thy courts is better than a thousand;*          PSALM
*I had rather stand at the threshold of the house of my God,*   84:11
*Than to dwell in the tents of wickedness.*

You might think that this last sentence is a common-
place, but it's very skillfully intimated that "Even if I
stood at Your door and was not admitted, I would
rather stand there than be admitted into the inmost
councils of the worldly and the wicked."

VAN DOREN:   Yes, "I'd rather be just on the
fringe of Your domain than at the heart of another."
I suppose the line, "A day in Thy courts is better than
a thousand" means "a thousand elsewhere."

SAMUEL:   "A thousand days or a thousand
years in any other place."

VAN DOREN:   In the King James Version of
the Book of Psalms I read as a child, there were, of
course, many, many sections in the whole work that I
missed. Maybe it was assumed that as a child, I
couldn't understand them—and that might have been
true. But in that version, the passage you just cited
runs differently: "I had rather be a doorkeeper in the
house of my God, then to dwell in the tents of wickedness."[44]

SAMUEL: The point of that translation would be, "the *least* in *Your* service is higher than the highest in the service of others."

VAN DOREN: "Stand at the threshold of the house of my God" I think is more powerful, because more extreme, than being a doorkeeper. Being a doorkeeper suggests that there was some kind of function or usefulness for him there.

SAMUEL: You've noticed in these expressions of supplication that the Psalmist does not ask for worldly reward, for position or for glory. When the prayers become most intense, what he is asking for most frequently and most insistently is specifically guidance. *He wants to be moral!* He wants God to teach him His way, and he is confident that once this has been given to him, then nothing can harm him. In other words, the acme, the culmination of human power lies not in the possession of strength, but in the security of knowing that he's following the right path.

VAN DOREN: Yes, and from having been in the position of being separated from God by an immense gulf (which he suggested that he was in, in those psalms of despair), and now to have reached the position of standing at the threshold is to have come a very great distance. That is why, perhaps, having suffered despair, it is enough for him now to be merely at the threshold. Merely *being* there is enough.

SAMUEL: The climax of the supplication occurs in Psalm 71, I think, when he says at one point:

*Cast me not off in the time of old age;*
*When my strength faileth, forsake me not.*

I'm sure he's not speaking there of being looked after, of social security. He means: "Don't let me in my old age forget You. Don't let my mind forsake You. Don't let my appreciation of You, and my contact with You fade away, but let me always have this knowledge of the relationship between us." That, perhaps, is the most painful thing for a man to contemplate: that he will reach an age when he is really no more alive, not being in contact with God.

VAN DOREN: Yes, and that is asking not merely that God keep remembering *him,* but that he be able to keep on remembering God.

# X

## "CONTRITION" *vs.* "REMORSE"

SAMUEL: In our last talk, Mark, we were speaking of the swing—the dramatic, the crucial swing —from despair to supplication, supplication being in fact inherent in the kind of despair which expresses itself, and doesn't become morosely silent and impotent. I would say that a concomitant of supplication is confession and contrition. Whether it precedes, psychologically, or whether it accompanies the renewal of belief, there must be a change in the supplicator. He must realize that whether or not it was for guilty acts that he was cast down into the pit, he has something to confess, and confession goes along with supplication.

VAN DOREN: We actually encountered a very great example of confession earlier in these talks [ *see pp. 36–37*] when we considered Psalm 51, David's confession of repentance after his sin with Bathsheba. But that was only one of several such instances in the Book of Psalms. The others, I take it, don't need to relate to any individual. Once more, I think, we can have a sense that the person speaking is speaking for anyone else.

SAMUEL: The psalms abound with *national* confessions, as it were. The people feels that it has sinned—as indeed it has. It's been taken back; and then again it has defected, and again it has gone back to supplication and contrition. The interchange of person and people in the psalms is very marked indeed.

VAN DOREN: In my opinion, Maurice, we're referring now, of course, to the ultimate dimension in poetry or in literature, in art of any sort. The greatest art is not about its maker, but about its audience. The greatest poem is not about its writer, but its reader. Ultimately, the poem succeeds only if it is true for everybody else, as well as for the person who wrote it. These days we hear a lot about the lives of poets; we're invited to read their biographies and to study their special psychologies, and so forth—as if their poems were interesting because they were about themselves. If a poem is really interesting, it's about *everybody* in the world!

SAMUEL: I'm very glad to hear you talk about that. It's rather unexpected, and I'm going to take advantage of it. I've been in a lot of discussion with people about the modern way of interpreting novels and poems in terms of the writer's life, as though you would understand the final significance of a piece of writing if you knew the writer. Whereas, what you're saying, it seems to me, is the very opposite: that unless that poem or novel becomes detached from the personal circumstance and becomes a universal—irrespective of what the writer had gone through—then it is not great literature.

VAN DOREN:    I believe that absolutely. I think all discussion of the lives of writers—as if those writers had sacred importance—is nonsense. It's even worse than nonsense!

SAMUEL:    Well, they may form studies by themselves. Not long ago a book appeared on Marcel Proust, in which the biographer said, "What do they know of *Remembrance of Things Past* who only *Remembrance of Things Past* know?"[45] My feeling is, in reading this great work of Proust's, and other great works to which I'm very much addicted, that if you've got to know what the author went through, then it isn't literature—it's a case history. And very often modern books are written like case histories.

VAN DOREN:    Exactly. I know that in my own case, if I may speak of it, nothing ever gives me more pleasure than to hear someone say of something that I've written, "That's true for me, too. I didn't know that anyone else had ever had that experience."

SAMUEL:    Or to hear someone say, "That's

what I've been trying to say all my life, and here I've found it!"

VAN DOREN: Yes!

SAMUEL: That's certainly true of the Bible. You read passages which prompt you to think, "Yes, that's what I wanted to say!" You may be reading it for the tenth or the twentieth time, but suddenly you realize all over again that this is what you wanted to say. But we have to get back more intimately to the Book of Psalms. When I spoke a moment ago of confession and contrition, I wanted to go on to ask your views on the question of the difference between "confession," or "contrition," and "remorse."

VAN DOREN: Ah, "remorse"! A terrible name for a terrible thing! It is that state which makes us cease to be able to consider anything except ourselves; indeed, it blinds us to everything except ourselves. We almost fall in love with our sins as we continue to contemplate them.

SAMUEL: Yes, we're frozen in a kind of perpetual horror, out of which we can't move. We keep on looking at and magnifying it, and dramatizing ourselves: "What a horrible thing! I shall never get over it!" Whereas, I take it, "contrition" is a genuine turning to the future in the light of one's past mistakes. The "broken and contrite heart" of Psalm 51 doesn't magnify its own villainy. Very often, a man in what we call "remorse" falls into a sort of stupor of self-admiration: "Oh, the tremendous sin I've committed!" Now actually, he is not an important person, and his significance is not cosmic. He has to understand that when he gets over it, he will find himself in a condition in which there flows from him a will to goodness which wipes out the past.

VAN DOREN:   Yes, but the past must be forgotten in those cases. I think we've all had the experience of wishing that someone of our acquaintance could forget the evil that he has done, because—as you said—it was not cosmic after all. If that person could forget the evil that he did, it would cease to exist.

SAMUEL:   Yes, I suppose the advice we might give such a person would be, "Don't make such a tremendous fuss about yourself, either in piety or in sinfulness, too."

VAN DOREN:   Psalm 32 details a very brilliant and refined analysis of the condition which makes confession, or contrition, good; because, to be sure, not to be able to confess, or not to be *willing* to confess, is to keep something inside of one that will do damage. Now we have just been saying that to continue to confess forever, to continue to moan and lament over one's evil, is to do damage to oneself, too. It's that old "Agenbite of Inwit."[46]

SAMUEL:   Yes, the "remorse of conscience"; the repeating and repeating and repeating again this self-analysis, and this self-scrutiny. It's a repetition of the word "remorse," which means "to bite again."

VAN DOREN: From the Latin *mordere,* "to bite"; and *re,* "again." As a matter of fact, we use that same idea these days when we ask about someone, "What's eating him?"

SAMUEL: Shakespeare got across the thought of gnawing in his phrase, "worm of conscience."[47]

VAN DOREN: But as I was going to say, Maurice, Psalm 32 analyzes the condition that precedes confession:

> *When I kept silence, my bones wore away*      PSALM
> *Through my groaning all the day long.*      32:3–5
> *For day and night Thy hand was heavy upon me;*
> *My sap was turned as in the droughts of summer.*
> *I acknowledged my sin unto Thee, and mine iniquity have I*
>     *not hid;*
> *I said: "I will make confession concerning my transgressions*
>     *unto the Lord"—*
> *And Thou, Thou forgavest the iniquity of my sin.*

In other words, while he was unable to confess, or while he had not been able to bring himself for any reason to that point, he was, as it were, destroyed within. And the implication is that the confession will now cleanse him. And you've been suggesting to me —and I'm very glad that you did because it throws a flood of light upon everything—what he will be cleansed of, among other things, is the very memory of his transgression.

SAMUEL: The memory and the feeling of importance. There's a whole literature of remorse. Books have been written about crimes that men have tried to repent of, and they have been unable really to repent because they were concentrating upon the horrendousness of the crime, instead of on the element of rebirth which is in them. I would say that Marlowe's *Doctor Faustus* is an instance of that kind. You remember that passage when he raves, *"O lente, lente currite noctis equi,* Run slowly, slowly, horses of the night,"[48] and he thinks there is no forgiveness. He is such a tremendous sinner! You see, that is the arrogance of some sinners, when they say, "This sin is so big that God can't forgive it!" Now that is not merely a blasphemy—it's a piece of megalomania! That *I* can commit a sin which even *God* can't forgive! That is actually making a god of yourself, the counterweight to the Great Forgiver!

VAN DOREN:    You spoke of Doctor Johnson in our last talk, Maurice. One reason that I love the old man is that he did something on a certain day which is highly pertinent to our subject right now. When he was a boy, he had once been disobedient toward his father, and the memory of that stayed with him for many, many years. The father was a bookseller in the English town of Lichfield, and he kept stalls in neighboring villages as well. It seems that one day young Sam refused to help his father at the Uttoxeter market. He remembered that refusal for forty or fifty years. Toward the end of his life, when he was an old man and famous, Doctor Johnson walked over to Uttoxeter, and stood bareheaded for a long time on the very spot where his father had kept his stall in the market. He said, "In contrition I stood, and I hope the penance was expiatory."[49] To me, that's a very moving story.

SAMUEL: It reminds me of another story about him—you mentioned fame, and that's what touched it off. An old acquaintance of Doctor Johnson's who hadn't seen the great man since schooldays one day confronted him on the street, shook hands with him, congratulated him on the fame that he'd achieved, the works he'd written, and said to him, "You know, Doctor Johnson, I too wanted to become a philosopher like you, but I always found my natural cheerfulness breaking in."

*(laughter)*

And Johnson couldn't forget that remark! He repeated it to Boswell, and Boswell recorded it.[50] Johnson was a very religious man, as you know.

VAN DOREN: Oh yes, very! There's something so *clean* about this incident of atonement. I think he might have said to himself, "Look here, I have let this disobedience eat on me, or bite on me, too long. It is wrong to suffer any more. I will tear this thing out of me."

SAMUEL: Have you noticed, Mark, that very often men will attach to some insignificant misdeed—one might say almost misdemeanor—of their childhood a whole weight of guilt? They make it symbolic of the guilt which pursued them through life. In his *Confessions,* Augustine, for example, remembers how, at the age of sixteen, he and his friends went out one night and stole pears from a tree near his home. And as a grown-up man, he remembered it. He burst into

tears, saying, "I didn't want those pears. I didn't need
them. I didn't even eat them. I stole them because I
wanted to steal!"[51] That youthful incident became for
him symbolic of all that is in a man of the purely
wicked: he wants to do a wicked deed for its own sake,
almost idealistically, not because there is any significance or reward whatsoever attached to it. Now I take
it that the Psalmist manages to liberate himself from
that crushing weight, that *Alpdrücken,* that nightmare
of guilt in which he is immobilized. Whatever it is that
holds him in its bondage—and it may not be one of the
important crimes of his life—the Psalmist is trying to
break loose from it.

VAN DOREN:    You speak of the trivial sin. If
I may be personal again, I remember that when I was
a student living at home in Illinois—perhaps I was
eighteen or twenty years old—one evening when I
was working up on the top floor of our house, where
I had a kind of study to myself, I heard my father
coming upstairs. He came up the first flight of stairs,
and the second to the third, and clearly, he had come
up merely to talk to me. I was alone up there; he was
alone for some reason downstairs. The rest of the
family were away, and he wanted to talk to me. He
came into the room where I was working—very much
absorbed, I dare say, in something, homework, or
reading, or writing—and I didn't hold a conversation
with him. I just went on reading. I said, "Hello," you
know, and a few casual things, but I didn't give him
what he wanted, namely, some conversation, probably
about what I was doing. I think he wanted to know
what I was doing.

SAMUEL:  You clammed up.

VAN DOREN:  I clammed up. I waited, and he went downstairs again. There was nothing overt about this. It was just a failure on my part to respond to a very natural and loving desire on his part. I didn't forget that for forty years. I finally wrote a poem about it,[52] to cleanse myself of it, and something happened then that interested me very much—we were referring to it a minute ago. A good many people have since said to me, "That happened to me once, too! I'm very glad you put it into words. It helps me now to know that someone else made that apparently slight mistake, and yet it assumed importance."

SAMUEL:  Yes, these are slight mistakes.

VAN DOREN:  They are omissions.

SAMUEL:  Omissions, or let us say, it is some commission, but very often acts of commission happen to bear the identity mark of some particular failing of ours, and though trivial in themselves, they have become a perfect expression of some particular lack in us —perhaps a kind of misdemeanor that we frequently repeat—so that they've become symbolic, and we concentrate on them erroneously, and yet with a certain reason. But Mark, you've led again into one of the characteristic aspects of confession in the Book of Psalms: what the Psalmist wants is to learn to go in the right direction. He addresses himself to God:

PSALM
32:5–8
*I acknowledged my sin unto Thee, and mine iniquity have I
not hid;*
*I said: "I will make confession concerning my transgressions
unto the Lord"—*
*And Thou, Thou forgavest the iniquity of my sin.*

*For this let every one that is godly pray unto Thee in a time
when Thou mayest be found;*
*Surely, when the great waters overflow, they will not reach
unto him.*
*Thou art my hiding-place; Thou wilt preserve me from the
adversary;*
*With songs of deliverance Thou wilt compass me about.*

And then, in quotation marks, because it's God who
is replying:

*"I will instruct thee and teach thee in the way which thou
shalt go;*
*I will give counsel, Mine eye being upon thee."*

That is to say, what the Psalmist is always asking for
is: "Tell me what I should do." It doesn't mean that
he's waiting for a literal instruction, "Do this, or that!"
but "Fill me with the outlook, or put me in the attitude
in which I will naturally do what I ought to do." This
is the burden of his prayer.

VAN DOREN:    And the desire for that can be
so strong that the Psalmist can be sick, as it were,
because he does not have his desire. In Psalm 38 there
is a really very piercing cry concerning his state because he has not yet confessed:

PSALM
38:3–9
*For Thine arrows are gone deep into me,*
*And Thy hand is come down upon me.*

*There is no soundness in my flesh because of Thine indigna-*
*   tion;*
*Neither is there any health in my bones because of my sin.*
*For mine iniquities are gone over my head;*
*As a heavy burden they are too heavy for me.*
*My wounds are noisome, they fester,*
*Because of my foolishness.*
*I am bent and bowed down greatly;*
*I go mourning all the day.*
*For my loins are filled with burning;*
*And there is no soundness in my flesh.*
*I am benumbed and sore crushed;*
*I groan by reason of the moaning of my heart.*

Now that might seem excessive, even hysterical, yet I
think for the Psalmist, it is not.

SAMUEL: Well, at one point it is. This is again
part of the despair and the turning point. But notice
how it goes further on:

*. . . I am as a deaf man, I hear not;*                          PSALM
*And I am as a dumb man that openeth not his mouth.*     38:14–15
*Yea, I am become as a man that heareth not,*
*And in whose mouth are no arguments.*

That is to say, before this clarification or loosening
takes place in him, he's panic-stricken, frozen, immobilized, unable to address himself to the business of
living.

VAN DOREN: And yet he's able to go on in
that same psalm:

*For in Thee, O Lord, do I hope;*                               PSALM
*Thou wilt answer, O Lord my God.*                            38:16

He cannot doubt it finally. And yet, until the answer comes, and until he has achieved the sense of being cleansed, he is in this really very dreadful state.

SAMUEL:   These psalms of contrition and of cry for guidance often make me think of a lack in modern life of a return to these sources. We have all sorts of psychological devices, mental therapy and psychoanalytic schools of various kinds. All of them evade or consider irrelevant the question of a man's relationship to God; or, if I'm not to put it into that too intense and, to some people, archaic form, a relationship to the forces of the world. The man is merely *handled*. A psychoanalyst or a psychologist inquires about this and about that; there's no question of a—let me put it almost on a low level—a life philosophy. No! It's all technical adjustment: "You've remembered this, you've forgotten that. Look at this and look at the other, and from now on, you'll be adjusted!"

VAN DOREN:   And of course, there is that term "guilt complex."

SAMUEL:   I've got a particular aversion to it—

VAN DOREN:   So have I.

SAMUEL:   . . . because of the glibness with which it's used. And so, for that matter, do I have an aversion to that word "adjusted." Who wants to be adjusted? What's the point of being "adjusted"?

VAN DOREN:   Let me answer that question. The Psalmist wants to be adjusted.

SAMUEL: Ah, yes! Of course he does! But with him, there is the emphasis on the word "just"! And with the modern technicians, the emphasis is on "adjust"!

VAN DOREN: I was only joking, of course. All the Psalmist's longing is to be adjusted to something so huge that not to be adjusted to it is to be nothing. Whereas, when we talk about adjustment nowadays, usually it's adjustment to a very little thing: the present world, or the city of New York.

SAMUEL: Oh yes! So that you'll never have any night sweats of having done something wrong— after you are "adjusted." You'll never have the embarrassment of having made a social *faux pas.* You'll just gurgle along like Elsie the Cow, and presumably you will give milk in abundance, Grade A milk —that is the ideal! It is disheartening, because there are things to which we should *never* be adjusted!

VAN DOREN: Of course!

SAMUEL: There are situations in which it is wrong for a man to be calm and take it with the detachment of a philosopher and of a thrice-psychoanalyzed patient. When the Psalmist speaks of God giving him peace, or strength, and protecting him, certainly it is not for the purpose of being able to go around throughout the world, saying, "I'm all right!"

VAN DOREN: Yes, "I have no problems!"

SAMUEL:   He *wants* his problems, problems
that will be here with us until the coming of the Messiah—unless, I don't know, the Messiah is going to be
the biggest problem of all!

VAN DOREN:   Well of course we want problems, but they had better be insoluble ones, because
we want to keep on asking questions that can't be
answered. There's no sense in asking a question that
*can* be answered. That's not an interesting thing to do.

SAMUEL:   And most of the great problems of
life of individuals are constituted by situations that
don't get answered, but get outlived. You pass beyond
the stage in which this is a burning reality for you, and
you see it from a distance. Then you say, "I've gone
through that phase." There's been no direct point-to-
point answer, but only a transcendance of it into the
next phase of your development.

VAN DOREN:   Maurice, we promised our-
selves last time that we were going to start on the way
up to those mountain peaks of peace and praise that
are at the end of the Book of Psalms—at least for us,
at any rate.

SAMUEL:   You mean we're a little ponderous
for people who are going to rise to new heights?

VAN DOREN:   No, or at least, I hope not.

SAMUEL:   But the turning point is difficult.

VAN DOREN: Yes, but the turning point, I think, is behind us. We are already on the way up because the experience of confession, as we have suggested, is the experience of being cleansed of that despair which did mark the bottom. We're well on the way up and are within reach of that wonderful free, open mood of thanksgiving and rejoicing which I hope that we can begin to express vicariously in our next talk. It's a mood of thanksgiving to God for delivering us, not only from outward enemies, not only from adversaries and those who attack us and lie in wait to kill us and speak harsh and untrue words against us—but from ourselves.

SAMUEL: You mean from our *worst* enemies.

VAN DOREN: Yes, our very worst enemies, who are ourselves.

# XI

# TOWARD
# THE GREEN PASTURES

SAMUEL: I'm rather glad we've passed through the dark phase of the Book of Psalms—the parts having to do with the valley of the shadow of death, and men's despair—and we're now coming into what I think of as the green pastures, the sunny foothills of the heights.

VAN DOREN: Which are so good to arrive at because of the depths out of which we've come. We would have done this book a great injustice, I think, Maurice, if we had endeavored to represent it as a group of pleasant little poems.

SAMUEL: You're quite right. Many people have the impression that the psalms are things to be

turned to—I won't say carelessly, but almost offhand-
edly—for recreation; whereas, as I think we've tried
to show, these are deep and terrible probings into the
human soul, and they were written, as it were, in
blood. And when we come to those parts where the
ecstatic begins to prevail over the depressed, it's still
obvious that here a man is piercing to the very inmost
chambers of his being in order to extract the secrets of
his feeling. Now that we're going to consider the expressions of peace, of thanksgiving and praise, it is, all
the same, a relief after the darkness of the former
material.

VAN DOREN:   The theme of thanksgiving, of
enormous relief in the spectacle of God's consent after
all to rescue the Psalmist out of the pit, is best stated
for me at the beginning of Psalm 92:

> *It is a good thing to give thanks unto the Lord,*          PSALM
> *And to sing praises unto Thy name, O Most High;*          92:2–4
> *To declare Thy lovingkindness in the morning,*
> *And Thy faithfulness in the night seasons,*
> *With an instrument of ten strings, and with the psaltery;*
> *With a solemn sound upon the harp.*

SAMUEL:   That rings through you, doesn't it?

VAN DOREN:   Yes. The mention of musical
instruments is very important, because many of the
psalms were intended to be chanted or sung to the
accompaniment of music.

SAMUEL:   I've often wondered, Mark, how
old musical instruments of the most primitive kind are.

I imagine that very, very early, before recorded history, people found they could pluck a taut string, maybe one that was crossed across a bow, and they observed that it gave forth a musical note. Or they blew into a shell and noticed that it gave notes; or they put a hollow reed to their lips and produced a pleasant sound. I suppose that before even language was developed thoroughly, they found it gave them some sort of lift to hear and to be able to produce these varieties of tones. Music and the dance, too, must be among the very, very oldest of human forms of expression. At the beginning of the Bible, Jubal is already mentioned as "the father of all such as handle the harp and pipe." Miriam, the sister of Moses and Aaron, led the women in singing and dancing after the children of Israel had crossed the Red Sea (or the Sea of Reeds,[53] as it is called in the latest translation). You remember David dancing before the Ark, in the ecstasy of his relief and joy that he was bringing it up at last to Jerusalem. As a matter of fact, singing and dancing as part of the religious ritual are specifically mentioned in Psalm 149:

GEN. 4:21

EXOD.
15:20

II SAM.
6:14

PSALM
149:2-3

> *Let Israel rejoice in his Maker;*
> *Let the children of Zion be joyful in their King.*
> *Let them praise His name in the dance;*
> *Let them sing praises unto Him with the timbrel and harp.*

I've always been struck by the desire of man to express his emotion not simply in words, but in the motion of his body, and in the manipulation of sounds through exterior objects.

VAN DOREN:   Music and dance are certainly among the oldest—as well as the newest—forms of human expression, and the human ingenuity in devising musical instruments keeps on. I visited the West Indies a few years ago where I was especially interested to see and hear the steel bands. As you perhaps know, the West Indians have taken advantage in comparatively recent years of the appearance in their islands of oil drums, those metal barrels in which oil is stored. They cut them off and beat the tops of them into wonderful musical instruments, on which they can play many, many notes.

SAMUEL: I've not been there, but I have heard some very primitive forms of music in central and southern Africa. I've seen Africans there use hollow coconut shells into which they had bored holes. A human being makes music out of anything. Of course, here in the Book of Psalms, there's already a highly sophisticated and advanced music. Throughout the psalms we have indications that there were instructions given to the choir and to the musicians.[54] Readers are often baffled by the headings, "For the Leader," which appear at the beginning of a number of psalms. Psalms 4, 5, and 6, for example, have that heading. These were the instructions to the Levites, as they stood on the Temple steps, or as they were assembled in the Temple courts: "This is the form of the music, and this is the form of instrument or instruments you will use," and the words accompanied them. Thus, Psalm 4 is to be accompanied by string-music; Psalm 5 by music on the *nehiloth,* or wind instruments; and Psalm 6 again by string-music, but specifically on the *sheminith,* which is supposed to have had a low, deep tone.[55]

Mark, Psalm 92 which you cited a moment ago,

is a very powerful example of thanksgiving. I like to revert to Psalm 18 as an extraordinary expression of this theme. That psalm appears with certain variations in Second Samuel 22, interwoven with the narrative of David's life, so that it has a double authenticity as belonging to David. The heading reads:

PSALM 18:1

*For the Leader. [A Psalm] of David the servant of the Lord, who spoke unto the Lord the words of this song in the day that the Lord delivered him from the hand of all his enemies, and from the hand of Saul; . . .*

(Incidentally, I don't know what that phrase, "in the *day*" means, since there wasn't *one* day on which David was rescued from Saul, or certainly from all his enemies. I suppose the reference is to the day when David made up his mind to give thanks in this particular form.) The psalm declares:

PSALM
18:2–7

*I love thee, O Lord, my strength.*
*The Lord is my rock, and my fortress, and my deliverer;*
*My God, my rock, in Him I take refuge;*
*My shield, and my horn of salvation, my high tower.*
*Praised, I cry, is the Lord,*
*And I am saved from mine enemies.*

*The cords of Death compassed me,*
*And the floods of Belial assailed me.*
*The cords of Sheol surrounded me;*
*The snares of Death confronted me.*
*In my distress I called upon the Lord,*
*And cried unto my God;*
*Out of His temple He heard my voice,*
*And my cry came before Him into His ears.*

There's a burst of joy and of triumph!

VAN DOREN:   At that point, we arrive at the beginning of what I regard as a very dramatic dream —a dream of how God rescued him. I'm always greatly moved by this, not merely because it's eloquent and brilliant in its expression, but because of the way it seems to answer a very deep yearning for the experience of deliverance. Now when I say "dream," I don't mean "delusion," or that thing for which we have the absurd name "wish-fulfillment."

SAMUEL:   You mean the visionary condition of a man.

VAN DOREN:   Exactly. Here's a complete vision of the deliverance taking place:

*Then the earth did shake and quake,*
*The foundations also of the mountains did tremble;*
*They were shaken, because He was wroth.*
*Smoke arose up in His nostrils,*
*And fire out of His mouth did devour;*
*Coals flamed forth from Him.*
*He bowed the heavens also, and came down;*
*And thick darkness was under His feet.*
*And He rode upon a cherub, and did fly;*
*Yea, He did swoop down upon the wings of the wind.*
*He made darkness His hiding-place, His pavilion round about*
    *Him;*
*Darkness of waters, thick clouds of the skies.*
*At the brightness before Him, there passed through His thick*
    *clouds*
*Hailstones and coals of fire.*
*The Lord also thundered in the heavens,*
*And the Most High gave forth His voice;*
*Hailstones and coals of fire.*
*And He sent out His arrows, and scattered them;*

PSALM
18:8–16

*And He shot forth lightnings, and discomfited them.*
*And the channels of waters appeared,*
*And the foundations of the world were laid bare,*
*At Thy rebuke, O Lord,*
*At the blast of the breath of Thy nostrils.*

SAMUEL:    That's apocalyptic, isn't it!

VAN DOREN:    I thought of that. And it's an answer, in the imagination of the Psalmist, to that condition which we've been discussing in our last few talks—the condition which made him cry out:

PSALM 94:3      *Lord, how long shall the wicked,*
             *How long shall the wicked exult?*

In Psalm 18, the wicked are exulting no longer, because here comes the Deliverer—riding a cherub!

SAMUEL:    Passages of this kind occur in the apocryphal books and to some extent in the Book of Daniel, but they are not as beautifully written, by any means. Literature of this sort has been made the basis for all sorts of mystical sects, which try to interpret these ecstatic outpourings into literal pictures of what the world scene is like. To me, this is a very grave mistake.

VAN DOREN:    Yes, I find it very dreary on the whole.

SAMUEL:    I'm thinking of examples in Swedenborgian and Gnostic literature generally, which has taken hold of these poetic images and has tried to turn them into a kind of plan for the structure of the universe: "This is where this happens, and this is where that happens. The arrows mean this, and the thunder means that." It's a pedantry of the mind which takes away the poetical significance of it.

VAN DOREN: Yes, it's something that could not have been done by people with imagination, I should say; whereas in Psalm 18, a glorious imagination goes just far enough. It gives us just enough, not too much. Always in those other things, we get too much.

SAMUEL: Notice how the Psalmist mingles this tremendous, world-shaking imagery with the homeliest kind of gratitude, which turns God from the mighty, the illimitable, and the ungraspable into what they now call with some derision, "the father image."[56] I don't know why people should do that: that God is the Father of all mankind is a very beautiful thought, but it is quoted at us often very mockingly, "Oh, you're thinking of the bearded man in the sky!" There again, by the way, is this literal interpretation of what was a poetical image. Psalm 30 contains one verse, apropos this relationship with God, which is peculiarly appealing to me:

*For His anger is but for a moment,*  PSALM 30:6
*His favour is for a life-time;*
*Weeping may tarry for the night,*
*But joy cometh in the morning.*

VAN DOREN: That's wonderful!

SAMUEL: Yes, it is. It is really humanity as the offspring of God, the creature of God, turning back to Him with a simplicity and homeliness which is altogether different from those moments when the Psalmist bursts into the *shiggayon,* the dithyrambic cry.[57] All of a sudden he becomes just an ordinary human, and infinitely pathetic.

VAN DOREN: That joy that came for him in the morning, he continues to celebrate through Psalm 30. At the end, you notice, he says:

PSALM<br>30:12-13

*Thou didst turn for me my mourning into dancing;*
*Thou didst loose my sackcloth, and gird me with gladness;*
*So that my glory may sing praise to Thee, and not be silent;*
*O Lord my God, I will give thanks unto Thee for ever.*

You're right: the joy is real, the joy is practical.

SAMUEL: There's a peculiar difficulty noticeable in the psalms. Very often you get the impression that the Psalmist is—I won't say stammering, but he's reached the limit of the possibility of human expression. For example, in Psalm 91, one of the most famous of all the psalms, he retreats suddenly into a kind of dark joy, if one may put it that way. The Psalmist sees God as the infinite, the all-mighty, and at the same time, longs to be close to Him. We, the infinitesimal, trying to identify ourselves with the infinite!

VAN DOREN: Psalm 91 is a perfect thing—the beginning of it, at any rate. For our purposes, it's absolutely apposite now:

> *O thou that dwellest in the covert of the Most High,*          PSALM 91:1
> *And abidest in the shadow of the Almighty; . . .*

SAMUEL:   Let me interrupt, Mark. You've just read nineteen English words, constituting the first verse of Psalm 91. In Hebrew, that verse has exactly *six* words. It goes like this:

| Yoshayv | besayter | elyon |
|---|---|---|
| *Thou that sittest* | *in the secret place* | *of the Most High* |
| betsayl | Shaddai | yitlonon |
| *in the shadow of* | *the Almighty One* | *he will rest (or abide)* |

It's very beautiful in the English. That strikes you at once. But in the Hebrew, it's all there, compact, in six words! I'm sorry for interrupting.

VAN DOREN:   No, I'm very glad you pointed it out. In other words, in English we get the same effect by scattering little words apparently on the page; whereas in the Hebrew, I imagine, you have six rather long and rather complicated words.

SAMUEL:   In this case, they don't happen to be long words, but they are highly condensed. The subject and verb and object (if the object happens to be a pronoun) can be drawn together into a single word.

VAN DOREN:   Let me come back to the English of Psalm 91:

> *O thou that dwellest in the covert of the Most High,*          PSALM
> *And abidest in the shadow of the Almighty;*          91:1–4
> *I will say of the Lord, who is my refuge and my fortress,*

*My God, in whom I trust,*
*That He will deliver thee from the snare of the fowler,*
*And from the noisome pestilence.*
*He will cover thee with His pinions,*
*And under His wings shalt thou take refuge; . . .*

There's the image of the wings again.

SAMUEL: All the imagery that you refer to—
the sensuous things, the things feelable and observable
—carry the idea home without intellectual ingenuity.

VAN DOREN: The entire psalm continues in
that way, but I think nowhere better than at the beginning, where the snare of the fowler, the pestilence, the
wings, the covert where one can hide—all come with
terrific concentration.

SAMUEL: Verse 5 of Psalm 91 has that marvelous phrase, *pakhad lylah,* which is "terror by
night." The verse reads: "Thou shalt not be afraid of
the terror by night." There's no reference to anything
specific—that the person is going to be attacked, or,
say, if it's the king, that there is going to be some kind
of insurrection. It's merely that in the night, sometimes there comes over you a horror of the world at
large. You don't see anything; you are a little unit in
the gigantic, infinite sphere which has its center everywhere and its periphery nowhere. The human being
is fearful because he's lost in the immensity of the
universe. And God will tell him, "I'll remove that
terror from you. Thou shalt not be afraid of the terror

by night." And then the psalm goes on to physical things:

> *Thou shalt not be afraid of the terror by night,*
> *Nor of the arrow that flieth by day;*
> *Of the pestilence that walketh in darkness,*
> *Nor of the destruction that wasteth at noonday.*

PSALM
91:5–7

> *A thousand may fall at thy side,*
> *And ten thousand at thy right hand;*
> *It shall not come nigh thee.*

VAN DOREN:   Yes—thou shalt be safe!

SAMUEL:   I'm sure that above all, what is referred to here is the sense of security. Having this assurance and this relationship, he walks with his head erect, knowing that no harm can befall him. Even if danger surrounds him, "it shall not come nigh thee" —that is, it won't penetrate to him.

VAN DOREN:   And think of what comfort came into the mind of the author of this poem at the very end, when he mentions God Himself speaking, and telling how He will deliver those who love Him. The Psalmist puts these words into God's very mouth:

> *"Because he hath set his love upon Me, therefore will I deliver*
> *him;*
> *I will set him on high, because he hath known My name.*
> *He shall call upon Me, and I will answer him;*
> *I will be with him in trouble;*
> *I will rescue him, and bring him to honour.*
> *With long life will I satisfy him,*
> *And make him to behold My salvation."*

PSALM
91:14–16

As I say, think what comfort that implies, against the background of those other psalms which we've been discussing, in which the Psalmist doubts that God is listening to him. He is even afraid sometimes that God has turned away from him!

SAMUEL:   This is the alternation, the swing-back. I always remember with pleasure a very simple Yiddish poem that conveys this same mood. It has a particular Hasidic flavor. As you probably know, Mark, Hasidism was a movement in which the ecstatic side of the psalms and of the Bible generally came to utterance—not in Hebrew, but in Yiddish. That's a language which is about eight-tenths Germanic; the remainder is mostly Hebrew and some Slavic.[58] But in the process of evolving this language called Yiddish, the Jewish people managed to transform it completely so that Yiddish is altogether different from German. The people poured into this language the intimate side of the psalms and of prayer generally. The exponents of Hasidism spoke, prayed, and thought in Yiddish, and Hasidism is peculiar in its homey approach to the Almighty.

VAN DOREN:   I should like to hear that poem.

SAMUEL: It's very short:

*Az Got iz mayn foter, vos hob ikh tsu zorgn?*
*Git er mir haynt nit, git er mir morgn.*
*Git er nit morgn, heyst er mir borgn.*

VAN DOREN:   I almost did understand that from German.

SAMUEL: The translation runs like this:

*With God as my father, why should I sorrow?*
*He won't give today, He'll give me tomorrow.*
*And if not tomorrow, He'll tell me to borrow.*

VAN DOREN *(laughing):* That's wonderful!

SAMUEL: There's a man perfectly at peace. Things are going to work out! Now it isn't what I would call a sloppy kind of optimism, namely, "Oh, God will provide. I don't have to do a thing!" This is almost gay. A man is in trouble, and he says, "Well, I won't get it today, I'll get it tomorrow!" He goes on working, and there's a cheerfulness in it which warms you—a cheerfulness which you find in these particular moods in the psalms.

VAN DOREN: Was that written by anybody that you know?

SAMUEL: I'd like to tell you the author's name, but to my great sorrow, I can't remember it, and I can't trace the poem. I don't know anymore whether it's a folk song.

VAN DOREN: Well, if he's a true poet and happens to learn that you've quoted him, he'd really be glad now that you didn't know his name. There's nothing more moving than the spectacle of a poem which completely says something for its own sake. The person who wrote it could take satisfaction merely in having his words quoted again by someone who thoroughly understood them, and who is grateful for them. It doesn't make any difference finally.

SAMUEL:    It has the sound of a folk poem, hasn't it?

VAN DOREN:    Yes, indeed!

SAMUEL:    As though it hadn't been written, but instead had just grown up, and nobody knows the real origins.

VAN DOREN:    And it's very hard to write that kind of poem, if you set out to do it!

SAMUEL *(laughing):*    It's very hard to write *any* kind of good poem! To try to imitate a folk poem particularly is out of the question. You'll come up with something which is obviously phony.

VAN DOREN:    Maurice, my curiosity is aroused by a verse in Psalm 116, in which the Psalmist gives specific thanks to the Lord for saving him. The line appears, I would say, apropos of nothing that he has been saying:

PSALM          *Precious in the sight of the Lord*
116:15         *Is the death of His saints.*

Now the verse before this doesn't lead up to that thought; and the one after it doesn't lead away from it. Has it ever interested you?

SAMUEL:    Yes, I've looked at it. It seems to be disjointed, apparently, from the other verses, but as you've observed, the thrust of the entire psalm gives thanks to God for having saved the life of the speaker.

The Psalmist is thinking, perhaps, in this verse, that if something happens to him, if he has to give up his life for his faith, it isn't just an empty gesticulation. He will testify in the presence of the people that God *does* see men being martyred, He *is* looking. These are to Him very precious incidents and very dear lives. If you like, you can even put it in a secular way: "If I am dying on earth for a principle, it isn't in vain!"

VAN DOREN:   Oh, I see! That makes all the difference to me. I think I hadn't realized that the "saint" here is almost synonymous with "martyr."

SAMUEL:   The Hebrew word in the text here that is translated as "His saints" is *hasidov.* The singular is *hasid,* and the plural is *hasidim.* (By the way, the Hasidic movement, or Hasidism, got its name from this same Hebrew word.) Other translations would be His "pious" or "godly" or "faithful ones." Among the traditional interpretations of this verse is one that gives this verse a different twist of meaning. Instead of

*Precious in the sight of the Lord*          PSALM
*Is the death of His saints*          116:15

some of the rabbinical commentators understood it as "Grievous in the sight of the Lord. . . ." In other words, the lives of the righteous are dear to Him. It is painful to God to have to tell the righteous that they must die—as He had to tell Moses, for example.[59]

VAN DOREN:   Oh well, that makes it perfectly clear, and I think it is not out of focus there, after all. Maurice, I suppose Psalm 136 sums up our whole discussion, and conveys the mood of thanksgiving and of joy that we have been commenting on. It starts:

PSALM
136:1–5

*O give thanks unto the Lord, for He is good,*
*For His mercy endureth for ever.*
*O give thanks unto the God of gods,*
*For His mercy endureth for ever.*
*O give thanks unto the Lord of lords*
*For His mercy endureth for ever.*

*To Him who alone doeth great wonders,*
*For His mercy endureth for ever.*
*To Him that by understanding made the heavens,*
*For His mercy endureth for ever.*

SAMUEL: You can actually *hear* that being sung, with the reader giving the first line, and the choir of Levites and all the people joining in the refrain, "*Ki le-olam chasdo,* For His mercy endureth for ever!" The reader goes through the tremendous events of the past, and every two or three seconds, the burst of music comes from the psalteries and the ten-stringed instruments, the cymbals clash, and the mass of the people shout, "For His mercy endureth for ever!"

# XII

## THE CAPACITY FOR SERENITY

SAMUEL: Mark, we had a good time—at least *I* had a good time, I hope you did—speaking of the grace and the cheerfulness of many of the psalms which are concerned with peace, thanksgiving, and general gratitude for the wonders of life.

VAN DOREN: Oh, I did!

SAMUEL: I hope every person has moments when he reflects, "How marvelous life has been to me!" If there are persons who never get that feeling, they must be very unhappy indeed.

If I may be personal, Mark, I've often thought what an astounding thing it is that I should be alive now at my age, when in advance, all the chances were

against me.[60] I was born in a country—Rumania—
where infant mortality was very high. My mother bore
nine children, of which three died in infancy. If I had
remained in Rumania, I would not have lived until
now, I am quite sure; many of the Jews of Rumania
perished during the Nazi occupation. My family
moved to England, where I went to school and later
managed to go to college. I came to America, served
in the Army in the First World War, and though I was
sent to the front, nothing happened to me—I was
withdrawn from it very soon. I've traveled a great deal
—by planes, ships, horseback, camelback—nothing
ever happened to me! And I look back upon it and I
say, "Why on earth should I have been one of the
spared persons?" Here I am, still at it! In these psalms
of thanksgiving we've touched on, the Psalmist has
that same mood: "Why, look what a break I've had!
What a thousand breaks I've had!" That makes him
want to sing out, "Oh, this couldn't have happened by
accident. Somebody must have been watching over
me!"

VAN DOREN:   Of course, Maurice, you are
very well aware of the danger of boasting about this,
so that you're not boasting, are you? You're not making any claims?

SAMUEL *(laughing):*   I don't know. Maybe I
was!

VAN DOREN:   No, no, I don't think you were.

SAMUEL:   The only claim I'm making is that I've been extraordinarily lucky!

VAN DOREN:   That's a very different thing, and being grateful for that is a very different thing from beginning to assume that somehow, good luck is your *due.*

SAMUEL:   Oh, yes, now I see what you mean. I've observed two kinds of people in this world: the first, if you do them a favor, immediately think that they deserve it; the second, if you do them a favor, are a little bit surprised and delighted, and feel that they're under an obligation to do a favor either to you or to someone else. This mood of God having been good to one, and making one for that reason feel secure (not in the sense of being immune from danger, but rather, in having been given the chances) breaks through in what I suppose is *the* most famous of all the psalms—the twenty-third:

*The Lord is my shepherd; I shall not want.*          PSALM 23:1

Isn't that a beautiful beginning—serene, secure, grateful; and apropos of your remark, I think quite without boasting.

VAN DOREN:   Yes, of course. I merely wanted to point out the very deep difference between gratitude and complacency—gratitude for favors done is a solemn thing. It recognizes that they *are* favors, given not because they were due, or deserved, or not because there was any obligation to give them; but

they were freely given. What is freely given is something to be grateful for—and to be surprised at, too.
Maurice, do you agree with me that Psalm 23 is the
one psalm out of the 150 psalms that most people can
recite?

SAMUEL:   When I said "*the* most famous," I
suppose I had that in mind, yes.

VAN DOREN:   One very short verse is important to us at the moment:

PSALM 23:3            *He restoreth my soul. . . .*

The reference there is not merely to good things given
from the outside—food, water, comfort, oil, and favor
—but also good done *within* me: "He restoreth my
*soul.*"

SAMUEL:   Yes, it is the counterpoint to what
goes before:

PSALM            *He maketh me to lie down in green pastures;*
23:2–3           *He leadeth me beside the still waters.*

And then:

*He restoreth my soul;*
*He guideth me in straight paths. . . .*

VAN DOREN:   Or, as it is sometimes translated, "paths of righteousness."

SAMUEL:   As we've remarked before, there's
always an eager, almost an anguished cry: "Teach me

the right way to live. Show me what to do!" This is his most insistent, most clamorous request to God.

VAN DOREN:    So that the Lord is represented here not only as a friend and a guide, but literally as counselor or teacher. Incidentally, at the very end of this very great poem, the translation we are consulting renders the text:

> *Surely goodness and mercy shall follow me all the days of my*     PSALM 23:6
> *life;*
> *And I shall dwell in the house of the Lord for ever.*

I've become aware recently that in other translations —newer ones—"for ever" is not there. Instead, phrases like "as long as I live" are substituted.[61]

SAMUEL:    No, "for ever" properly belongs there. The Hebrew phrase is *le-orekh yomim,* "for length of days," and there is the poetic sense there of prolongation and completeness.

VAN DOREN:    I'm glad to hear that, because certain modern translations end something like this: "for a long time," or "for many years." These versions seem to me to be anticlimactic, to say the least. But one thing I'd like to get clear is: the phrase doesn't mean "for ever *in eternity*"?

SAMUEL:    There's no implication there of eternity. The Psalmist is saying, "I shall be wrapped up in this grace of Yours for the whole of my life."
    This is a remarkable kind of serenity, Mark— this man who feels that he is surrounded by a great

Force, who fears nothing, and who is confident that he will be forever secure, for his entire life. Do you think that such serenity can be attained without some such belief as is indicated in the Book of Psalms? There have been great, serene personalities outside of the faith—nonbelievers in personal immortality and nonbelievers also in a God who has a direct interest in them. One such serene person was Socrates, and another was Marcus Aurelius. They didn't believe that there was a personal relationship between them and the Creator of the universe, did they?

VAN DOREN:    Socrates at least liked to refer to the *daimon* or "familiar oracle" who counseled him and taught him. He told the court in Athens: "You wonder where I get some of my ideas. From whom, if anybody, have I learned what I think I know, namely that I know nothing. I have a *daimon* which comes to me."[62] And of course, Marcus Aurelius referred to a thing he called "Nature."[63] It was not a god or goddess in the ordinary sense of that term, and yet it existed outside of him, and his endeavor was to live harmoniously with it, as if that were a job, and not an easy job at that.

SAMUEL:    But predominantly, I would say that Marcus Aurelius felt that one achieved security by living in harmony with the laws of nature, with—you might call it "the soul of the world." But it isn't the same thing we have in mind, is it?

VAN DOREN:    No.

SAMUEL:   Living in harmony with the laws of nature is almost a scientific concept, isn't it?

VAN DOREN:   Yes, it is. Now it's a very interesting question that you've asked there. I've often thought about it. I dare say that it's ultimately true that serenity and peace of mind are not possible unless there is the faith that something of an immense, eternal sort, and a Person, too, exists, who gives sense to serenity. And yet I agree that there are people who seem to have it anyway. My answer to your question might be this: serenity of the complete sort maybe is never possessed by anyone who doesn't have *in addition* to his faith the *capacity* for serenity. You know, there are people who pay lip service to God; who piously say that they believe in Him, and go through all the motions—attending churches and synagogues, performing rituals, and what-not; and yet who still do not strike us as having "restored" souls. It hasn't done them any good.

SAMUEL:   We actually see many people who have what might be called faith. They believe in God, a personal God, but they are tormented souls just the same. We've seen that mood in the Psalmist. He hasn't lost his faith when he's in those miserable moods; and there are people in whom these moods are the consistent tenor of their lives.

VAN DOREN:   I would say that the person who has in some genuine sense a serenity of soul has to have, among other things, what I call the innate capacity for it. Somewhere within his very being he must

have the capacity to become serene, with the help, to
be sure, of something outside himself. But he also goes
to meet that something at least half way. Does that
make sense?

SAMUEL:   Indeed it does. I was going to lead
from that to another question that rises in connection
with these psalms of security and well-being: the modern psychological use of security. A person mis-
behaves, and people rush forward to say that he mis-
behaved because he's "insecure." Then, when they
talk of making him feel secure in order to counteract
these wayward, immoral impulses, they confine themselves completely to the "adjusting" of the person.
(We touched on this word, Mark, in an earlier talk
[see p. 158] but the subject is especially pertinent here.)
The notion of a security based on, or at least accompanied by, some such conception as we've been discussing is entirely absent. Now I'm not saying that
psychologists should become ministers and rabbis—
although there is a whole area of religious activity
today where clergymen devote themselves to "pasto-
ral counseling." What I object to is that psychology as
such pays only lip service—if it ever does!—to the idea
of faith; and believes that it's all a technical question.
"Move certain complexes, certain memories, get the
man integrated with such-and-such circumstances,
help him to adjust, and this sense of security will flow."
That, in my opinion, isn't security; it's a trick!

VAN DOREN:   The appearance of techniques
there is what gives it the shallow sound and feeling
that it has. I quite agree with you; people speak glibly

about the problem, almost as if they were saying that an operation could correct the condition.

SAMUEL: You know how it comes to me sometimes? I've wondered whether a man can be completely moral—completely, utterly moral—if he hasn't got a faith in God. I've been told, "Yes, there are such people." But my reflection has been this: if a man doesn't feel—at least at times—so strongly about morality that it leads him by excess of emotion into a belief in God, even if he hasn't got one, then I don't trust the substance, or the texture, of his morality. It's something that must lead one into a compulsive, poetic conception of the existence of God. In Psalm 46, this idea rises to tremendous utterance:

> *God is our refuge and strength,*        PSALM
> *A very present help in trouble.*          46:2–6
> *Therefore will we not fear, though the earth do change,*
> *And though the mountains be moved into the heart of the seas.*
> *Though the waters thereof roar and foam,*
> *Though the mountains shake at the swelling thereof.*

Then he breaks into this sweet new strain:

> *There is a river, the streams whereof make glad the city of God,*
> *The holiest dwelling-place of the Most High.*
> *God is in the midst of her, she shall not be moved;*
> *God shall help her, at the approach of morning.*

"There is a river, the streams whereof make glad the city of God"—now that's an utterance which bursts forth from the Psalmist spontaneously, and it illustrates what I mean. I would say that if a man's belief isn't strong enough to make him talk like that, then it

isn't full belief. In other words, if a man isn't compelled by the power of his emotion to speak of the
existence of God, and to acknowledge it, then the
emotion is not as deep as it ought to be, or can be, or
certainly as deep as it is here.

(Incidentally, Mark, notice that the second
verse is often misquoted. People often say "in time of
trouble.")

VAN DOREN:   Yes, it seems to me that I almost always hear it as "A very present help in time of
trouble."

SAMUEL:   The misquotation weakens it, because it takes away the force of the word "present,"
which means that it is "here" and it also means "at this
particular moment."

VAN DOREN:   The help is "here and now."
Maurice, that magnificent line, "There is a river," has
moved a great many people. I suddenly remember a
very famous scientific work of the nineteenth century,
a book on oceanography by a man named Maury.[64] A
paragraph in that celebrated book begins: "There is a
river that flows in the Atlantic Ocean." Maury there
is referring to the Gulf Stream, and that particular
sentence achieved fame on its own. It's a tribute to the
sheer literary power of the psalms.

SAMUEL:   This same spontaneous poetic outburst breaks through in Psalm 8:

*When I behold Thy heavens, the work of Thy fingers,*     PSALM
*The moon and the stars, which Thou hast established;*      8:4–10
*What is man, that Thou art mindful of him?*
*And the son of man, that Thou thinkest of him?*
*Yet Thou hast made him but little lower than the angels,*
*And hast crowned him with glory and honour.*
*Thou hast made him to have dominion over the works of Thy*
    *hands;*
*Thou hast put all things under his feet:*
*Sheep and oxen, all of them,*
*Yea, and the beasts of the field;*
*The fowl of the air, and the fish of the sea;*
*Whatsoever passeth through the paths of the seas.*

*O Lord, our Lord,*
*How glorious is Thy name in all the earth!*

When I read that, I wonder at the way people prattle
these days. They speak of the wonder which is awak-
ened in us by the scientific exploration of the universe,
of space travel; and of the investigations into the in-
tricacies and intimacies of the cell, and of forms of life;
and they say, "Now *that* teaches us how wonderful life
is!" Is it your impression that people are *more* aware
of the wonder of the world through these media than
the Psalmist was, without any of this detailed knowledge?

VAN DOREN:  No. No, I'm certain that the
contrary is the case. Nobody could have had the excitement, nobody now, I think, needs to be understood as feeling anything comparable to the author of,
say, Psalm 121:

PSALM 121     *I will lift up mine eyes unto the mountains:*
              *From whence shall my help come?*
              *My help cometh from the Lord,*
              *Who made heaven and earth.*

              *He will not suffer thy foot to be moved;*
              *He that keepeth thee will not slumber.*
              *Behold, He that keepeth Israel*
              *Doth neither slumber nor sleep.*

              *The Lord is thy keeper;*
              *The Lord is thy shade upon thy right hand.*
              *The sun shall not smite thee by day,*
              *Nor the moon by night.*

              *The Lord shall keep thee from all evil;*
              *He shall keep thy soul.*
              *The Lord shall guard thy going out and thy coming in,*
              *From this time forth and for ever.*

SAMUEL:   Oh, that is a marvelous utterance!

VAN DOREN:   And by the way, that's a reference not to a little man who stands by, helping us through doors, and so forth. It refers to a very great Person who occupies the whole world!

SAMUEL:   Those references in Psalm 8 and 121 to the moon and the stars and the sun remind me again of the moderns who are so eager to say, "What Copernican astronomy taught us is *humility!* The earth is not the center of the universe; it's not even the center of the solar system. Even the sun isn't the center of the universe; even the galactic system to which we belong isn't the center of the universe. Now, let *that* teach you humility!" And do you know what happens? A kind of competition in humility: "I'm more humble than you!" Jews have very many satiric stories about themselves, and one of them is apropos at this point. It concerns a great scholar who lay dying, a man of learning and piety, and his pupils were standing around his bed, already lamenting him—in his hearing. One of them said: "What an ocean of wisdom!" And another said: "What an abyss of understanding!" And another said: "What a sweep of vision!" And the dying man croaked: "Yes, gentlemen, and don't forget my modesty!"

VAN DOREN *(laughing)*: "The mountain of my modesty!"

SAMUEL: That's it! Now this continuous competition among moderns today is ludicrous. They tell us, "Those old people"—meaning the Psalmist and the men who wrote the Bible—"didn't know what humility was because they thought themselves at the center of the universe."

VAN DOREN: There's a paradox there. I think we've lost our modesty. In that very act of realizing that we're *not* the center of the world, we've lost our humility. When we *were* the center of the world, or thought we were, the pressures of all the world were upon us; the eyes of all the world were literally upon us. Everything that we did was seen, everything we thought was significant; and we had a kind of responsibility to the universe and to eternity which could make us humble. Now that we are free, now that we are swinging around in some minor orbit, we have to manifest our importance to ourselves. We have to say, "Sure, we're nothing in particular!" but we must make out that, after all, because we're conscious, we are great.

SAMUEL:   This is what Bertrand Russell implies in his thinking on the subject. He says that man stands alone in the universe, and we have the courage and the power to throw back, as it were, the chill and the despair of infinite space. Now this is a kind of bragging.[65] To be sure, ancient man bragged; man has always bragged. But this feeling of not having any responsibility at all is something new—and this is the essence of what you've just been saying: "We have no responsibility! We're not the center of anything! Here in some obscure and utterly insignificant corner of space, which is infinite, some little thing called human beings crawl around upon some miniscule planet!" Either we are crushed with despair, and we summon a humility which is the inverse of arrogance (you know, a man saying to himself: "Isn't it marvelous of me to realize how insignificant I am!"); or else we go to the other extreme and say, "I defy the universe!"

VAN DOREN:   Well, many absurd things are said, and I find it makes far better sense to get back to the Psalmist. We've been speaking of the peace and the serenity which the individual person can find. I've always been touched by Psalm 133, which talks about the happiness and the pleasure, too (I insist on using both of those words) of knowing that one is a member of a *community* of happy persons:

PSALM 133        *Behold, how good and how pleasant it is*
                 *For brethren to dwell together in unity!*

*It is like the precious oil upon the head,*
*Coming down upon the beard;*
*Even Aaron's beard,*
*That cometh down upon the collar of his garments;*
*Like the dew of Hermon,*
*That cometh down upon the mountains of Zion;*
*For there the Lord commanded the blessing,*
*Even life for ever.*

"How good and how pleasant it is for brethren to dwell together in unity!" Maybe the ultimate dimension of peace is that which comes with the sense that joy is shared, that joy is not an individual possession, clutched to some single breast.

SAMUEL: Of course it isn't. To have a joy that one can't share is hardly a joy at all. And in the last analysis, if you haven't someone personal around to share it with, well then, you share it with God—that is the concept. But here, the notion is the reinforcement of a man's life by the interweaving of it with the rest of the community. This falls in with the profoundest impulses and significances in the Jewish religion. Judaism teaches that it is in the community and as part of it—in the choral effect, if you want, of communal life—that the greatest music is produced. The greatest music is not the solo of a man's own voice.

VAN DOREN: Yes, the choral effect is what I had in mind. These wonderful psalms of praise that we are now coming to as the grand climax of the Book of Psalms are collective utterances, all the voices singing together!

# XIII

## OF HUMILITY AND PRAISE

SAMUEL: Before we move from the psalms which communicate the idea of peace, calm, and a sense of direction, even when there seems to be chaos in the universe, to those which are luminous with praise, Mark, let me touch once more on that marvelous passage:

PSALM
126:5

*They that sow in tears*
*Shall reap in joy.*

I ask myself sometimes: is it necessary to "sow in tears" in order to "reap in joy"? Is there no bliss in fulfillment if first we don't labor, sweat, and agonize?

VAN DOREN: You're asking me a pretty big question to answer on the spot. I would say that in all probability, there *is* a necessary connection between the two. Spinoza once remarked that every good thing is made with great trouble;[66] and we could add there —with great effort, too. That's true of any work of art, of the world that was created, of the birth of a child. Every living person started in an agony of effort on the part of his mother and himself.

SAMUEL:   He came out crying! I ask that, not just for the general philosophic examination of that question, but for something else. Nowadays, there's a feeling that any kind of frustration is bad. The psychologists have a kind of watchword: "Frustration leads to aggression!" The implication is, if you take away frustration, there won't be any aggression. Now, supposing you were to rephrase that in simple, straightforward language: "Give a man what he wants, and he'll never be angry," the logical consequence of which is: "Give a man whatever he wants!"

VAN DOREN:   "And never cease to do so!"

SAMUEL:   Yes! This is what issues for me as a question from this examination of "They that sow in tears": isn't there such a thing as *creative* frustration? Isn't frustration a necessary and a welcome thing, a necessary part of the human drive?

VAN DOREN:   I don't think it's ever *desired.* Anyone would like to do whatever he does easily. And it's true that some great things *are* done easily, and quickly. I think sometimes these days—at least in the field of the study of art—we tend to magnify the importance of effort, or at any rate, of visible effort. In my opinion, the greatest of all musicians is Mozart, and he seems not to have had the slightest difficulty in writing anything that he ever wrote.

SAMUEL *(laughing):* Well, those are the blessed geniuses! When people say that the highest form of art is to conceal art, that doesn't mean there wasn't any art, any labor, put into it. You've got to conceal the effort—but the effort was there!

VAN DOREN: Yes, that's true, but if the works of Shakespeare, for instance, had presented themselves to him as problems, he could never have solved them. No amount of effort could have written *King Lear* if he hadn't had the genius. And the man who wrote *that* wrote thirty-six other plays. It's utterly unbelievable.

SAMUEL: By the way, some of them are quite rubbishy, aren't they?

VAN DOREN: Some are better than others.

SAMUEL *(laughing):* I wouldn't put it that way. I'd say some are *worse* than others! I think, for example, *The Merry Wives of Windsor* is a pretty sloppy piece of work. Don't you think so?

VAN DOREN: It's not interesting. Well, say thirty, then, instead of thirty-six. No one ever did anything like that, and he did it so easily, and his contemporaries were bitter because he did it easily.

They sweated and roared and boomed and bellowed about how difficult it was—but it was not difficult for him, any more, I suspect, than it was difficult for the Psalmist to write the psalms.

SAMUEL:  Do you think that they came fairly easily?

VAN DOREN:  I suspect so.

SAMUEL:  Well, sometimes I have my doubts about that. I imagine that even Shakespeare had his problems. He is out of this world, as we say, almost in the sense that the Bible is, and perhaps he abused the divine gift that was given to him. You remember it was said of him that "he never blotted out a line." and a critic commented, "Would he had blotted a thousand."[67] We may be divided on this point, Mark. He was just too careless! He scattered with a prodigal hand!

VAN DOREN:  It doesn't make any difference. My point is this: we don't know whether the Psalmist had difficulty or not. In the absence of any evidence, I think it's just as likely that he had no difficulty as that he had great difficulty, because it is true in the realm of art that the difficulty is not of any very great importance in itself. It isn't what makes the work good. The thing that counts is what's *in* it!

SAMUEL:  Maybe it's that a man has to struggle in order not to let too much dross accompany the gold. But when you move from the sequences of the psalms of serenity into the field of praise, there is more evidence for what you're saying. Praise itself doesn't come out as an effort. It's something which is spontaneous, and more than that, it's irrepressible. A man gets up and just wants to shout, "Hallelujah, I'm alive!" It takes the form of all these marvelous variations in the psalms; it takes the form of praise of God. Actually, praise belongs to nobody but God; one should not praise anyone but Him.

VAN DOREN:    In a way, one never does praise anyone but God. We compliment one another; we offer one another tribute of that sort. But there's nothing more absurd than to imagine "complimenting" God. One praises Him, because He is the ultimate recipient of whatever praise is. It's in His completeness, in His complete abstraction that we find the reason for calling Him God. When we praise one another, rather than compliment one another (and, of course, we do praise great men), we're not praising anything personal in them, but rather, qualities in them.

SAMUEL:    Yes! Or at least, one should. One should try to avoid inflating the ego of the person. Just recently I came across a statement by the nineteenth-century English clergyman, Sydney Smith, who was such a wit. He said something which is very pertinent and sharply put: "Among the smaller duties of life, I hardly know any one more important than that of not praising where praise is not due."[68] You know, we want to be nice to people, and so we follow the general notion in the book, *How to Win Friends and Influence*

*People*—I forget the author's name, and he'd better be forgotten, I think. His idea was, "You *praise* people."

VAN DOREN:   Yes, you make everybody feel good.

SAMUEL:   It doesn't matter a hang, apparently, whether the praise is deserved, or it isn't. It's like those masters of ceremonies on TV and radio programs, "Give the little girl a big hand!" before she's performed, so that it will make her feel good and inflate her and go on from there.

VAN DOREN:   Many people thinking of the psalms offhand—and indeed, they would include me —would consider them as substantially and at their center poems of praise of God. The great thing about them is that the praise is of course due to the subject. That's an understatement. The praise is so due, so necessary for those who want to give it, that they cannot restrain themselves. That is where the effect of spontaneity comes in: they sing praises unto God *as if they couldn't help it!* They are overcome with their desire to do it. They want to do it *not* to make God feel good, because I'm sure their conception of Him is lofty enough to understand that they are praising Him not because He wants it, or needs it, or has asked to be praised. But it is a noble thing to praise. It's the sign of greatness in anyone when he can praise.

SAMUEL:   I. L. Peretz, one of the three classic Yiddish authors in modern times, has a charming story about this.[69] He describes a young Jew arguing with

his father. The son says: "Wouldn't you get sick to the
stomach if a man went around telling you to your face,
'You are a wonderful tailor. You are a marvelous
tailor. You are the only tailor!' Wouldn't that make
you sick?" The old man says, "Yes, it would." The son
goes on, "Well, now, don't you think it makes God
sick to hear all of this adulation poured out at His feet
three times a day?" The old man meditates on this, and
suddenly bursts out, "You're absolutely right. But a
man has to do it, hasn't he?" *A man has to do it!* The
son couldn't compel his father to share his view because he was falsely transposing that situation to the
merely human. If he had been talking only about human beings, the young man would have been right.
The Talmud has a saying: "A part of a man's praise
may be told in his presence. The whole must be said
only in his absence."

VAN DOREN:    Or after his death.

SAMUEL:    Now it's quite otherwise when you
want to chant in sheer exuberance of appreciation.
You flower out in gleeful happiness, "What a marvelous world it is, and how marvelous must be the Power
that created it!"

VAN DOREN:    That's it! There is something
compulsive about this praise; it just must be given. The
men who have it in them simply must let it forth. They
can't help themselves, and they tend to do it together.
It isn't one voice speaking in these psalms of praise; it
is many voices, I think, all praising God together, and
saying, for instance:

*Hallelujah;*
*For it is good to sing praises unto our God;*
*For it is pleasant, and praise is comely.*

PSALM
147:1

Praise is a lovely thing. Only distinguished people, of
course, are capable of praising. There are some persons, you know, who never can praise anybody or
anything. You probably have encountered such.

SAMUEL:   Yes, they are frozen; or sometimes,
is it the result of shyness?

VAN DOREN:   No, I think it's the result of
weakness. I'm less interested in Sydney Smith's fear
that he will praise someone who doesn't deserve it
than I am in someone who's afraid that he will not
praise someone who *does* deserve it.

SAMUEL:   Or some *thing,* rather, because you
said a moment ago, one praises a quality or something
produced. Yes, it is a grudging and hesitant spirit who
cannot praise; he won't let his feelings flow out of him.

VAN DOREN:   But the Psalmist is always
breaking forth:

*O Lord, our Lord,*
*How glorious is Thy name in all the earth!*
*Whose majesty is rehearsed above the heavens.*

PSALM 8:2

It's as if he were realizing it all over again! He looked
about him and he considered everything:

*Out of the mouth of babes and sucklings hast Thou founded*
*strength,*

PSALM
8:3–10

*Because of Thine adversaries;*
*That Thou mightest still the enemy and the avenger.*

*When I behold Thy heavens, the work of Thy fingers,*
*The moon and the stars, which Thou hast established;*
*What is man, that Thou art mindful of him?*
*And the son of man, that Thou thinkest of him?*
*Yet Thou hast made him but little lower than the angels,*
*And hast crowned him with glory and honour.*
*Thou hast made him to have dominion over the works of Thy*
    *hands;*[70]
*Thou hast put all things under his feet:*
*Sheep and oxen, all of them,*
*Yea, and the beasts of the field;*
*The fowl of the air, and the fish of the sea;*
*Whatsoever passeth through the paths of the seas.*

*O Lord, our Lord,*
*How glorious is Thy name in all the earth!*

SAMUEL:    It's an organ tone. You feel it peal-
ing down the aisle!

VAN DOREN:    It says actually a very complicated thing, too: "What is man, that Thou art mindful of him?" The speaker realizes how little he is,
being a man.

SAMUEL:    This is the humility, the genuine
humility, we were speaking of.

VAN DOREN:    And yet the Psalmist points out
that this little man who speaks thus to God, only one
of His many, many creatures, nevertheless, by some
decision of God (which the man at this point doesn't
seem to be able to understand, and maybe he

shouldn't try) has been placed over the other creatures
and given dominion over them. I love the fear and
trembling with which he accepts that responsibility in
these psalms.

SAMUEL: By the way, you spoke very cor-
rectly about the complexity of the idea, and that English translation, "a little lower than the angels," in-
troduces still another complexity. The Hebrew text
doesn't use the word "angels" at all, but rather, *Elo-
him,* meaning God Himself. Other translations I've
consulted render this verse "less than God," or "less
only than God."[71] To translate that "a little lower than
God Himself" would be in consonance with Jewish
thinking, because in their view, man, not the angels,
is the next stage below God. The angels, having no
power to do evil, don't share in the merit of doing
good. Those creatures which haven't the capacity to
choose—and the angels would fall into this category—
naturally don't get the credit for having made the
choice.

VAN DOREN: We may be only "a little
lower," yet still, we are a created thing. I'm fascinated,
Maurice, by the way the Psalmist sometimes repeats
phrases. It's as if he were a musical instrument. He
breaks out at one point:

*Sing praises to God, sing praises;*            PSALM
*Sing praises unto our King, sing praises.*      47:7–8

*For God is the King of all the earth;*
*Sing ye praises in a skilful song.*

The repetition of that phrase is to me particularly touching. But then, at other times, he develops a complicated idea, such as the one we just cited; or the one in Psalm 29, when the Psalmist seems to hear God expressing Himself. The very world is His voice:

PSALM
29:3–11

*The voice of the Lord is upon the waters;*
*The God of glory thundereth,*
*Even the Lord upon many waters.*
*The voice of the Lord is powerful;*
*The voice of the Lord is full of majesty.*
*The voice of the Lord breaketh the cedars;*
*Yea, the Lord breaketh in pieces the cedars of Lebanon.*
*He maketh them also to skip like a calf;*
*Lebanon and Sirion like a young wild-ox.*
*The voice of the Lord heweth out flames of fire.*
*The voice of the Lord shaketh the wilderness;*
*The Lord shaketh the wilderness of Kadesh.*
*The voice of the Lord maketh the hinds to calve,*
*And strippeth the forests bare;*
*And in His temple all say: "Glory."*

*The Lord sat enthroned at the flood;*
*Yea, the Lord sitteth as King for ever.*
*The Lord will give strength unto His people.*
*The Lord will bless His people with peace.*

SAMUEL: Tremendous! Why is it that we can't create a comparable modern scientific—what shall I call it?—dithyramb, dealing with the world? We've found out, presumably, how much more wonderful the world is than they knew three or four thousand years ago. Let us say this was written twenty-five hundred years ago. They didn't know about the atom and the subatomic particles; they didn't know that space is bent; and they had no idea of the infinite marvels that modern man has discovered in biology, in genetics, in mathematics, medicine, chemistry, and physics. Why haven't we got a comparable literature of astonishment? What is it that chokes us?

VAN DOREN:   We spend out time praising the men who discovered these things. We praise the scientist; we don't praise God who made both the world and the scientist. All this promotes in me a very curious reflection. The men who wrote the psalms proved their greatness by their capacity to understand how much greater than they Something or Somebody else was—namely, God. You see, what proves anyone's greatness is his capacity to recognize greatness in others. There may be a paradox in that.

SAMUEL:   There *is* a paradox, and it amounts to this: what's happening to modern man is, "How wonderful I am to understand all this!" Instead of having the attitude, "How wonderful *that* is . . .

VAN DOREN:   . . . to be understood by *me!"* Exactly!

SAMUEL:   Mark, among these psalms of praise is a very familiar phrase that's always impressed me, and I can't quite get the meaning of it in its literal sense. We've been talking about the way the Psalmist uses the three-dimensional, and the palpable, the obvious, the visible, in order to express intellectual ideas. What do you make of this verse:

> *Lift up your heads, O ye gates,*                    PSALM 24:9
> *Yea, lift them up, ye everlasting doors;*
> *That the King of glory may come in.*

The figurative meaning is clear there, but how do you literally understand "lifting up" the head of the gate? Was there some kind of mechanism that they had to lift up before the gate could be rolled back?

VAN DOREN:  I've read that psalm to myself many times, often in a room where I've closed the door because I love to thunder that psalm. And I never thought about its precise meaning until I was rereading the psalms for our discussions. I've looked up many commentaries on this particular passage. None is very satisfactory to me—I wish I had never consulted any of them! As far as I can gather, the "gates" referred to here seem to be those of the Temple.

SAMUEL:  But what does "lift up" mean?[72] A gate wasn't a curtain; there must have been some kind of device atop it which acted as a bolt. Once you've lifted up the bolt, the "head," then possibly you unlocked it, allowing the gate to be rolled back. But in any case, it makes a tremendous phrase:

PSALM 24:
7–10

*Lift up your heads O ye gates,*
*And be ye lifted up, ye everlasting doors;*
*That the King of glory may come in.*
*"Who is the King of glory?"*
*"The Lord strong and mighty,*
*The Lord mighty in battle."*
*Lift up your heads, O ye gates,*
*Yea, lift them up, ye everlasting doors;*
*That the King of glory may come in.*
*"Who then is the King of glory?"*
*"The Lord of hosts;*
*He is the King of glory."*

There's a proud, a magnificent chant going back and
forth: "Lift up for the King!" "Who is the King?"
"The Lord of the universe!"

VAN DOREN: That's one of my favorite
psalms. It always gives me intense, and even mysteri-
ous, pleasure, and I think formerly I may have had just
as good a notion as I have of it now that I've tried to
find out what it means to others. Because after all,
what a poem means to *you* may be just as important as
what it means to others. I think it used to mean merely
this: that the gates were addressed as living things,
thing that hear, things that could lift themselves.

SAMUEL: Apropos of that, something recurs
to me. Many years ago, I read one of the psalms without looking up the Hebrew. The verse, as it appears
in the King James translation, says:

> . . . *He giveth His beloved sleep.*

PSALM
127:2

I understood the word "sleep" there to mean the sleep
of peace; and I thought it meant, "He gives His peace,
which is so beloved, to someone." Then I looked up
the Hebrew and discovered that the literal reads:

> . . . *He gives sleep to His beloved.*

There still remains with me that first form, "He gives
His beloved peace," that is, His peace which is beyond
understanding," with "beloved" used as an adjective
modifying "sleep of peace"—and that form is very
precious to me. This corroborates your own view, that
whatever it means to you—if it has deep meaning—
was implicit in what the poet wanted to say.

VAN DOREN: Those misunderstandings—if that's what they are—are often times most creative things. Earlier [*see p. 188*], we mentioned how the verse, "A very present help in trouble" is so often misread as "A very present help in time of trouble." I spoke of this to a friend once, and he said, "Well, isn't that the way it is?" I got a copy of the Bible and showed him the line, and he said, "Oh dear, I suppose it is just a natural tendency of everybody who speaks English, at any rate, to ride an iambic pentameter line." Because that's what a misreading of that line comes out as: "A very present help in time of trouble."

PSALM 46:2

SAMUEL *(laughing):* A little too glib, isn't it?

VAN DOREN: Yes, it is.

SAMUEL: I mean, you'd have rejected that line yourself in one of your poems.

VAN DOREN: Oh, yes!

SAMUEL: It reminds me of Mark Twain's remark about Byron's famous line in his poem, *Destruction of Sennacherib.* You remember it: "The Assyrian came down like a wolf on the fold,/ And his cohorts were gleaming in purple and gold;/ And the sheen of their spears was like stars on the sea,/ When the blue wave rolls nightly on deep Galilee." Mark Twain said: "It sounds just like buttermilk gurgling out of a narrow-necked bottle!"

VAN DOREN *(laughing):* Well, now, the

psalms are great poems, and this comment is never true of *them*. For one thing, they don't contain any words that are just stuck in to fill out some form. Every word in them counts.

SAMUEL:   And every word is both inevitable and unpredictable.

# XIV

## ALL THE GLORY
## OF THE UNIVERSE

SAMUEL: We've been leading up to the great culmination, the immense diapason, one might call it, of the psalmodic mode—the great praises. It's very difficult to single out any one of the great *Hallels,* the psalms of praise, for comment because they are all so magnificent.

VAN DOREN: Specifically, of course, the last five psalms in the Book of Psalms begin with the word, "Hallelujah" and they are often so-called.[73] But the mood of praise, and the word, too, occur earlier. For example, Psalms 111, 112, and 113, open with "Hallelujah," and Psalm 104 closes with it. I've often remarked on the noble capacity of the writers of the Bible for remembering the creatures of the earth,

other than man, and in Psalm 104, we hear about "the
wild asses," "the fowl of the heaven," "cattle," "the
stork," "the wild goats;" and about "mountains," and
"grass" and "cedars of Lebanon," "fir trees," "high
mountains," and "rocks." At night, "the beasts of the
forest do creep forth." Then the Psalmist goes on:

> *The young lions roar after their prey,*
> *And seek their food from God.*
> *The sun ariseth, they slink away,*
> *And couch in their dens.*
> *Man goeth forth upon his work*
> *And to his labor until the evening.*
>
> *How manifold are Thy works, O Lord!*
> *In wisdom hast Thou made them all;*
> *The earth is full of Thy creatures.*

PSALM
104:21–24

SAMUEL:   Scientists tell us, Mark, that a tiny
plot of earth—say, a square foot—is filled actually with
millions of micro-organisms. I'm reminded of that
when the Psalmist says, "The earth is full of Thy creatures." It's not only in the visible, but in the invisible
realm: the earth is jammed with life. It overflows!

VAN DOREN:   And the Psalmist, in his genius,
somehow always is able to remember that. His isn't
just one lone quivering voice speaking in the wilderness. His voice is rising out of a chorus of voices, many
of which, shall we say, are unheard—but which might
be heard. He goes on:

> *Yonder sea, great and wide,*
> *Therein are creeping things innumerable,*
> *Living creatures, both small and great.*
> *There go the ships;*

PSALM 104:
25–35

*There is leviathan, whom Thou hast formed to sport therein.*
*All of them wait for Thee,*
*That Thou mayest give them their food in due season.*
*Thou givest it unto them, they gather it;*
*Thou openest Thy hand, they are satisfied with good.*
*Thou hidest Thy face, they vanish;*
*Thou withdrawest their breath, they perish,*
*And return to their dust.*
*Thou sendest forth Thy spirit, they are created;*
*And Thou renewest the face of the earth.*

*May the glory of the Lord endure for ever;*
*Let the Lord rejoice in His works!*
*Who looketh on the earth, and it trembleth;*
*He toucheth the mountains, and they smoke.*
*I will sing unto the Lord as long as I live;*
*I will sing praise to my God while I have any being.*
*Let my musing be sweet unto Him;*
*As for me, I will rejoice in the Lord.*
*Let sinners cease out of the earth,*
*And let the wicked be no more.*
*Bless the Lord, O my soul.*
*Hallelujah.*

That word "smoke" is tremendous! It's as if the very mention of God's power to touch them made them burst into flame. The vitality of these poems is unspeakable!

SAMUEL: You notice that phrase: "There is leviathan, whom Thou hast formed to sport therein." Say, it's the whale, flaying about with his tail in the waters, and he's having one marvelous time!

VAN DOREN: That's what he was put there for!

SAMUEL: The Hebrew verb, *lesah-chayk,* translated there as "to sport," really means "to play." In the popular tradition, Jews have made of leviathan a plaything. There's a legend that when the Messiah comes and the world ends, the Jews will be able to partake—among other things—of roast leviathan! At this great feast, every Jew will get a share of him, as well as of the legendary great ox; and to wash all of this down, they will drink of the bottles of wine which were put away from before the creation of the world. Just as leviathan plays around in the sea, the Jews have played around with the idea of leviathan. He's supposed to engirdle the whole of the earth in the submarine depths, with his tail in his mouth![74]

VAN DOREN: That's a wonderful idea! You know, the Psalmist in his ecstasy over his power to realize the extent and depth of life in the world, sometimes remembers that he does not, however, understand himself. He is one creature speaking, and yet— who is he to claim that he knows himself? At one point he suddenly says, rather quietly:

> *O Lord, Thou hast searched me, and known me.*
> *Thou knowest my downsitting and mine uprising,*
> *Thou understandest my thought afar off.*
> *Thou measurest my going about and my lying down,*
> *And art acquainted with all my ways.*
> *For there is not a word in my tongue,*
> *But, lo, O Lord, Thou knowest it altogether.*
> *Thou hast hemmed me in behind and before,*
> *And laid Thy hand upon me.*
> *Such knowledge is too wonderful for me;*
> *Too high, I cannot attain unto it. . . .*

PSALM 139: 1–6, 14

*I will give thanks unto Thee, for I am fearfully and wonder-fully made; . . .*

Think what's he's saying there: God has created all things, and He takes pleasure now in contemplating all these things; and in addition, He has knowledge of each individual thing, which the individual thing does not have of itself.

SAMUEL:   In the scientific world, Mark, which I admire and love and do my best to follow with my inadequate resources, there is an aversion to the idea of purpose in the universe. The word "teleology"— the doctrine that everything in nature was made for a purpose—is offensive to the scientists. All these marvels, as they seem to be to us; all of these things that seem to fit in one into the other, as the Psalmist portrays them, and as man feels them to be—all these are merely the result of an accidental interplay of the atoms. The whole course of human development, the human dream of a universe and of a Maker—all this, to those scientists, is nonsensical and irrelevant. They say that in nature itself, there is simply adaptation; and to speak of something having a "purpose" is to misunderstand nature completely. In their view, a man has no right to assert, for instance, that oxygen and hydrogen unite *to* form water, because that would imply that that is their purpose. One must say instead: "Oxygen and hydrogen unite, *and* they form water." To state it in that first way would be to commit the same foolishness as the eighteenth-century French chemist—I no longer remember his name—who was performing an experiment and showing off to the court at Versailles. He said to the king: "These two gasses will now have the honor of uniting before Your Majesty!" *(laughing)* Now modern scientists say that to speak of things having been created for man, or for anybody, is the same sycophancy as was demonstrated by this chemist. But to me, that view is nonsense.

VAN DOREN:   Yes, and by the way, I myself don't think that all things were created for *man.* I suppose you don't either, do you?

SAMUEL:   No, not for man. But there is a purpose, generally speaking; that I do believe.

VAN DOREN:   Because things were created for *themselves,* each thing, if you please, for itself. And that's why I love these memories that the Psalmist keeps having of other creatures. They exist in the same way that we exist. They have their pleasures, their food, their life, their death. They have their night, and they have their day, and it is a wonderful thing that all this keeps going on. I quite agree with you that the scientist—if that's what he does—explains nothing when he says, "It just happened." That's no explanation either, is it?

SAMUEL:   No. To say that something "just happened" is simply to say, "There it is." Mark, to return to these psalms, in his high moments of exaltation, the Psalmist is capable of reminding us of the vastness of God's presence in the universe, but also of His presence in the minutiae of creation. The contrast

of the macrocosmic against the microcosmic is remarkable. Now this is the macrocosmic view:

PSALM
139:7–12

*Whither shall I go from Thy spirit?*
*Or whither shall I flee from Thy presence?*
*If I ascend up into heaven, Thou art there;*
*If I make my bed in the nether-world, behold, Thou art there.*
*If I take the wings of the morning,*
*And dwell in the uttermost parts of the sea;*
*Even there would Thy hand lead me,*
*And Thy right hand would hold me.*
*And if I say: "Surely the darkness shall envelop me,*
*And the light about me shall be night";*
*Even the darkness is not too dark for Thee,*
*But the night shineth as the day;*
*The darkness is even as the light.*

This is the concept of the world in large.

VAN DOREN:   In contrast, Psalm 148 gets
down to detailed things. Notice, it isn't the Psalmist
who is praising things; he is asking each thing to praise
God:

PSALM 148

*Hallelujah.*
*Praise ye the Lord from the heavens;*
*Praise Him in the heights.*
*Praise ye Him, all His angels;*
*Praise ye Him, all His hosts.*
*Praise ye Him, sun and moon;*
*Praise Him, all ye stars of light.*
*Praise Him, ye heavens of heavens,*
*And ye waters that are above the heavens.*
*Let them praise the name of the Lord;*
*For He commanded, and they were created.*
*He hath also established them for ever and ever;*
*He hath made a decree which shall not be transgressed.*

*Praise the Lord from the earth,*
*Ye sea-monsters, and all deeps;*
*Fire and hail, snow and vapour,*
*Stormy wind, fulfilling His word;*
*Mountains and all hills,*
*Fruitful trees and all cedars;*
*Beasts and all cattle,*
*Creeping things and winged fowl;*
*Kings of the earth and all peoples,*
*Princes and all judges of the earth;*
*Both young men and maidens,*
*Old men and children;*
*Let them praise the name of the Lord,*
*For His name alone is exalted;*
*His glory is above the earth and heaven.*
*And He hath lifted up a horn for His people,*
*A praise for all His saints,*
*Even for the children of Israel, a people near unto Him.*
*Hallelujah.*

It's the chorus of praise from all living things!

SAMUEL:    Yes, it's the universe, not the earth alone. People speak of the music of the spheres, or of the music of being. This is the grand outburst of melody which I suppose every great composer has striven to reproduce. It's not a single voice rising up here; but the chorus of the omnipresent world, all of it realized in a sort of instantaneous moment of self-realization, and of God-realization.

VAN DOREN:    Sometimes when I'm driving through the countryside in the spring, I hear those little frogs called "peepers" that raise a chorus of sound particularly in the evening in March or April.

And I'll declare! it often seems to me as if they were
a chorus praising God, praising something, praising
life. They seem so happy, and yet they're down there
in the dark, damp, miserable swampy place. But
they're just ecstatic.

SAMUEL:   Of course—that's their home! They
wouldn't like to be in an air-conditioned room! I was
thinking: most people aren't aware of the at-homeness
of things in their particular circumstances. That's
where they belong, and their natural utterance is their
native relationship to being. I'm reminded of that old
philosophical problem all of us encounter in high
school or early college: supposing we weren't around
to hear sounds; would the sounds be there? In other
words, would the song of a bird be a song if there
wasn't an ear—our ear—to listen? The philosopher
George Berkeley in early eighteenth-century England
answered that question, of course, by saying that all
these things always exist in the mind of God; that we
ourselves exist in His mind; and that those things exist
whether we are there or not. In contrast to Berkeley,
there's another philosophic outlook, not necessarily
modern, which holds that these things are there only
because man experiences them. For example, the light
of the stars would not be the light of the stars if men
didn't see it; and the music of the waves would not be
music, inasmuch as there would be no ears for the
vibrations to impinge on, to be conveyed to some
brain which translates them into a psychic percep-
tion.

There always seems to me in that latter view a
sort of niggling egocentricity: "If I'm not around,

there ain't nothin'! As long as I'm around, the world exists. But the moment I disappear, all the glory of the universe has been wiped out!" Or, "If I don't appear, neither will all of this glory appear!" *(laughing)* And yet, this is what is called a scientific philosophic view. Now here is the Psalmist crying out:

> *Hallelujah.*                                                     PSALM 149
> *Sing unto the Lord a new song,*
> *And His praise in the assembly of the saints. . . .*
> *Let them praise His name in the dance;*
> *Let them sing praises unto Him with the timbrel and harp. . . .*
>
> *Let the high praises of God be in their mouth,*
> *And a two-edged sword in their hand; . . .*
> *To bind their kings with chains,*
> *And their nobles with fetters of iron;*
> *To execute upon them the judgment written;*
> *He is the glory of all His saints.*
> *Hallelujah.*

Well, if I weren't here, the Psalmist wouldn't have written that—or anything! That's what that scientific philosophic view is equivalent to. And if I don't exist, well then, Shakespeare, the Bible, and all the great men of the universe are merely delusions that I'm entertaining at present.

VAN DOREN:   And you could add: "In my pride, I can even believe that I created them!"—as scholars often believe that they create the authors they edit.

SAMUEL:   Yes, and as grammarians think that they created the rules of a language. Whereas the rules of a language are made by the people; and then the grammarians come and say very pompously, "Yes, that's right, and that's wrong."

VAN DOREN:    Among these great Hallelujah psalms at the end of the Book of Psalms, there is a line that suddenly erupts, as it were, out of a context that doesn't necessarily explain it. Although it doesn't make it wrong; as a matter of fact, the effect is magnificent:

PSALM
146:1–4

*Hallelujah.*
*Praise the Lord, O my soul.*
*I will praise the Lord while I live;*
*I will sing praises unto my God while I have my being.*

*Put not your trust in princes,*
*Nor in the son of man, in whom there is no help.*
*His breath goeth forth, he returneth to his dust;*
*In that very day his thoughts perish.*

Why does the Psalmist suddenly say, "Put not your trust in princes . . ."? That's a rhetorical question, Maurice.

SAMUEL:    No, it's a genuine question, Mark, as to why it occurs there. The magnificence of the divine conception is something that is remote from human standards. The human being is inclined to worship and to exalt earthly grandeur and earthly power. And when the Psalmist says there, "Put not your trust in princes," he means not simply, "Don't expect great things from them, and don't rely on their promises"; but more than that: "All this earthly glory is simply rubbishy. It's irrelevant; it's tangential to the reality. Forget all earthly glory and think only of the majesty of God!"

VAN DOREN: That's right. That is a perfect statement of it, and my question *was* rhetorical; it wasn't that I couldn't understand it. What I was really asking you to do was to contemplate this after a rather sudden transition from the vast object that he began considering to the little object.

SAMUEL: It's very possible that many other people who have contemplated this passage have come to other conclusions. You know, in the very old Jewish tradition, going back two thousand years and more, there is implicit in every verse of the *Tanach,* the Hebrew Bible, an infinitude of interpretations.[75] This is comprehensible because of something we referred to before: the incredible terseness of these statements. Many of them are distillations, apparently, of long processes of thought. Others might be compared to a proverb that has been wandering around among people, and in the process has gathered into it the essences of an infinitude of experiences. I suppose that this verse, "Put not your trust," suddenly coming in could be interpreted in a score of ways—and all of them would be valid. We'll never know what it was that the original writer intended.

VAN DOREN: However, your original explanation is borne out by what follows "Put not your trust in princes, . . .":

*Happy is he whose help is the God of Jacob,*
*Whose hope is in the Lord his God,*
*Who made heaven and earth,*
*The sea, and all that in them is;*
*Who keepeth truth for ever; . . .*

PSALM
146:5–6

No prince, of course, could do that; no prince, no "son of man" (the synonym for "prince" here). No prince could have made the heaven and earth, nor could "keep truth for ever." Only the Maker of the world, of course, could do that.

SAMUEL:    The Psalmist warns: *Al tiv'techu vin'- divim,* "Put not your trust in princes." The equivalent nowadays is something else. We put our trust in various things: in democracy, on the one side; in ourselves; but above all, we're putting our trust in the capacity of science to answer all of our problems. I wonder whether one can reinterpret this and say, "Yes, this is good. This has a purpose. But don't put your trust in it because the trust of man is to be confided to another source of much greater significance and depth."

VAN DOREN:    Very good, Maurice. I think the application is excellent. In other words, "Let's not put our trust in anything less than the All." That's the note which is sounded throughout the psalms, and that's the note on which the book ends in a great clash of cymbals, and with the voices of all living things praising Him:

PSALM 150      *Hallelujah.*
              *Praise God in His sanctuary;*
              *Praise Him in the firmament of His power.*
              *Praise Him for His mighty acts;*
              *Praise Him according to His abundant greatness.*
              *Praise Him with the blast of the horn;*
              *Praise Him with the psaltery and harp.*
              *Praise Him with the timbrel and dance;*

*Praise Him with stringed instruments and the pipe.*
*Praise Him with the loud-sounding cymbals;*
*Praise Him with the clanging cymbals.*
*Let every thing that hath breath praise the Lord.*
*Hallelujah.*

# ABOUT MARK VAN DOREN:
## AN AFTERWORD

I see Mark Van Doren with a double vision: through Maurice's eyes and my own. We loved him and delighted in him for the special kind of joy he always brought to our home. The doorbell would ring, and there was Mark, tall, lean, buoyant; the face seamed with lines of laughter and intense feeling, incredibly alive, fresh, youthful; the hair a white halo around that strong head of wisdom. Here was loving-kindness itself on our threshold!

Mark's effect on Maurice, even in absentia, was astonishingly visible and audible. Maurice would emerge gloomily from his workroom, say late of a dark winter's afternoon when the day's stint at the typewriter had yielded perhaps a single paragraph or a single line that had survived his severe self-criticism, and he would announce to me, "Remind me, in two hours I must call Mark." The merest mention of Mark's name lifted his spirits, for minutes later, over the sound of ripping paper, came Maurice's voice, humming. Half an hour later, he would emerge again, now smiling: "I'm going to take a little nap, but you must be sure to wake me to call Mark." In fifteen minutes, there he was, checking all the clocks in the house. "Why wait?" he'd say. "I'll call him now." And off he would go to his workroom, singing a little snatch of a Hasidic melody, a bar out of *Traviata*, or a line from the English music-hall of his Manchester youth. Silence now while dialing his friend Mark in Connecticut. A click, a pause, a great welling up of laughter, and Maurice's loud, joyous peal, "MARK! Is that you, Mark? How ARE you, Mark?" Then, his business transacted, and love communicated from house to house, Maurice would seek me out, always with the same gesture and comment. He would remove his horn-rimmed glasses, wipe the tears of laughter from his eyes, and say emphatically, "What a marvelous fellow, that Mark, absolutely marvelous!"

The last time Maurice ever laughed out loud was in the hospital, just a few days before his death. Mark had scribbled him a little note, which I started to read aloud. "Dear Maestro," Mark began, and I had to stop reading.

In the months between Maurice's death on May 4, 1972, and Mark's sudden passing on December 10, 1972, I was in frequent touch with Mark while I worked, under the burden of mourning, to finish *In the Beginning, Love.* Mark was the soul of kindness and of strength, never speaking of his own health, but expressing great delight in the project. In one of our final phone conversations, I remember telling him that I'd been rereading his 1969 collection of poetry called *That Shining Place.* Of all the poems in that book, the eleven he had called "Psalms" had touched me the most deeply. "You're not telling me that just to say something nice?" he asked. No, I replied, the language, the rhythm and progression of ideas affected me very much like the biblical psalms. Mark said that he had been uneasy. "I wasn't sure that I had the right to call them 'Psalms.' " I told him that some years ago, the gifted Canadian Jewish poet A. M. Klein (who died also in 1972; it was a bitter year!) had written a number of poems he had entitled "Psalms." Maurice at one time had even proposed that some of them be considered for inclusion in a revision of the Jewish prayerbook. No one, to my knowledge, had been offended by the use of that title. It was my own feeling that anyone endowed with the talent had the right to use the word. Mark breathed a sigh of relief. "I didn't want anyone to think I was presumptuous," he said. "I really intended them as my psalms."

Here are two of Mark's psalms, printed with the permission of Mark's beloved wife, Dorothy. I suspect that David himself would have treasured them and their author, as I do.

EDITH SAMUEL

## Mark Van Doren's Psalm 2

*He sings to me when I am sad.*
*His voice is old, but sweeter than honey.*
*It comes from farther off than I can see.*
*It is not the world singing, it is he*
*That made it, and he makes it once again*
*As way down here I listen,*
*Listen, and am sad once more*
*With so much sweetness,*
*Sweetness—O, my Lord, how can I bear it?*
*Yet bear it, says the song, and so I do,*
*I bear it, all that sweetness, as he has*
*Forever, says the song he sings to me.*


## Mark Van Doren's Psalm 3

*Praise Orion and the Great Bear,*
*Praise icy Sirius so burning blue,*
*Praise the slow dawn, but then the razor rim*
*Of sun that in another hour*
*Cannot be looked at lest it blind you; praise*
*Mountain tops, praise valleys, praise the silver*
*Streams that circle towns; praise people's houses;*
*Praise sitting cats that wait for doors to open;*
*Praise running dogs; praise women, men;*
*Praise little boys who think their fathers perfect;*
*Praise fathers who believe their Father perfect;*
*Praise him because he is, because he has*
*His being where no eye, no ear can follow,*
*No mind say whence or whither,*
*Yet he is, and nothing else is*
*Save as witness to his wonder,*
*Save as hungering to praise him—*
*Let all things, then, great or little,*
*Praise him, praise him*
*Without end.*

A Postscript

Edith Samuel has beautifully expressed the warm friendship between the Samuels and the Van Dorens. As for the scholar and poet, it was love at first sight and the attachment grew stronger for twenty years, until death divided them.

DOROTHY VAN DOREN

# NOTES

In the course of editing these dialogues, I compiled a sheaf of informal notes for myself on a number of topics—variant readings of certain passages, commentaries, historical background, legends, and the like. I am glad to make them available here for the general reader. The basic references consulted, and the abbreviations used here to identify them, are:

*Encyclopaedia Judaica* (Jerusalem and New York: Encyclopaedia Judaica and the Macmillan Company, 1972). Abbreviated here as *E.J.*

*The Book of Psalms for the Modern Reader,* a new translation by Gershon Hadas. (New York: Jonathan David, 1964). Abbreviated here: Hadas.

*The Book of Psalms:* A New Translation according to the Traditional Hebrew Text (Philadelphia: The

Jewish Publication Society of America, 1972). Abbreviated here: J.P.S. 1972 *Psalms*.

*The Torah:* The Five Books of Moses. A new translation of The Holy Scriptures according to the Masoretic text (Philadelphia: The Jewish Publication Society of America, 1962). Abbreviated here: J.P.S. 1962 *Torah*.

*The Legends of the Jews* by Louis Ginzberg in seven volumes (Philadelphia: The Jewish Publication Society of America, 1913). Abbreviated here: *Legends*.

*The Midrash on Psalms,* translated from the Hebrew and Aramaic by William G. Braude, in two volumes (New Haven: Yale University Press, 1959). Abbreviated here: *Midrash*.

*The Holy Bible:* Revised Standard Version. An ecumenical edition. (New York, Glasgow, London, Toronto, Sydney, Auckland: Collins, 1973.) Abbreviated here: *R.S.V.* The King James Version of 1611 is abbreviated here as: *K.J.V.*

*The Complete Bible:* An American Translation. The Old Testament translated by J. M. Powis Smith and a group of scholars . . . (Chicago: The University of Chicago Press, 1923, 1927, 1948). Abbreviated here: Smith.

*The Psalms:* Hebrew text and English translation with an introduction and commentary [by] the Rev. Dr. A[braham] Cohen (London: The Soncino Press, 1958). Abbreviated here: Soncino *Psalms*.

1   Rabbi Levi Yitzhak of Berditchev (1740–1809), one of the great Hasidic masters, was the author of the famous *Kaddish*—a demand to the Judge of the

universe to do justice—and of the equally famous
*Dudeleh,* or "Thou" song. In Yiddish, the title is
a play on words. *Dudeleh* means simply a "little
tune"; *Du* also means "Thou." In *Heritage of Music:
The Music of the Jewish People* (New York: Union of
American Hebrew Congregations, 1972), Judith
Kaplan Eisenstein presents English translations
and music arrangements of both songs. The English of *Dudeleh* is quoted here by permission of
the publisher. It goes in part:

> *Master of the Universe, I will sing You a dudeleh.*
> *Where can I find Thee,*
> *And where can I not find Thee?*
> *For where I stray, there art Thou,*
> *And where I stay, there art Thou—*
> *Only Thou, ever Thou, always Thou . . .*
> *In heaven Thou, on earth art Thou, above art Thou, below
> art Thou. . . .*
> *East art Thou, West art Thou, North art Thou, South art
> Thou. . . .*
> *Here and there and everywhere art Thou!*

Incidentally, for those readers interested in psalmody and in a modern reconstruction of ancient
Temple instruments, the method of chanting
psalms, and contemporary musical examples, *Heritage of Music* is heartily recommended.

2 *My Daily Psalm: The Book of Psalms Arranged for Each
Day of the Week,* ed. Rt. Rev. Msgr. Joseph B. Frey
(Brooklyn, N.Y.: Confraternity of the Precious
Blood, 5300 Fort Hamilton Parkway, n.d.). Fore-
word, p.vii. Quoted by permission.

3   The term "hallelujah" appears nowhere else in the
    Bible except in the Book of Psalms, and only in the
    last third of the book, beginning with Psalm 104.
    It was a liturgical expression used in the Temple as
    a signal to the congregation to respond. "Hal-
    lelujah-singing" was adopted by the Christian tra-
    dition from its earliest period. See entry, "Hal-
    lelujah" in *E.J.*, vol. vii; and *Heritage of Music,* pp.
    24–27.

4   In his Preface to *Paradise Lost,* John Milton scorns
    the use of rhyme as "being no necessary Adjunct
    or true Ornament of Poem or good Verse, in
    longer Works especially. . . ."

5   The Hebrew phrase *ishon aino* is understood to
    mean the pupil of the eye, and is so rendered in the
    J.P.S. 1962 *Torah* translation of Deut. 32:10 and
    the Hadas translation of Ps. 17:8. The *R.S.V.* re-
    tains the "apple" image from the old *K.J.V.* in
    both instances. Happily, the J.P.S. 1972 *Psalms*
    translation stays with the charming phrase, "the
    apple of Your eye" in Ps. 17:8.

6   Walter Pater, *Marius the Epicurean: His Sensations
    and Ideas.*

7   Blaise Pascal, *Pensées,* trans. W. F. Trotter (New
    York: The Modern Library, c. 1941), p. 81.

8   The image of "reins" and "heart" also appears in
    tandem in Ps. 7:10. Dr. Cohen in Soncino *Psalms*
    comments (p. 17) that in the Bible, the heart is the

seat of the intellect, and the "reins" (or kidneys) the seat of the emotions. In combination," he says, "they determine a man's character and actions."

9   "Reason Has Moons" by Ralph Hodgson (1871–1962) in his *Poems* (New York: Macmillan, 1917). Maurice was given a copy of this slender volume in 1918; I came across it for the first time in 1973 among his large and heavily dog-eared collection of books of poetry. Curious about Hodgson as a neglected poet, I looked him up in the *Encyclopaedia Britannica* and discovered the possible reason: Hodgson, a gifted English poet, "almost ceased to write" after 1917.

10  The differing meanings of the Hebrew word *ruach* were strongly impressed upon readers of the J.P.S. 1962 *Torah* translation at the very opening of the Book of Genesis. The familiar old translation of Gen. 1:2 (". . . and the spirit of God hovered over the face of the waters.") was replaced by ". . . and a wind of God sweeping over the water." Professor Harry M. Orlinsky, the distinguished Bible scholar who served as editor-in-chief of the *Torah* translation committee, has strongly upheld the "wind" translation, noting, among other things, that the same word, *ruach,* is used in Gen. 3:8. There God is moving about in the Garden of Eden at "the breezy time of day." Those interested in pursuing the matter may wish to look into *Notes on the New Translation of the Torah,* ed. Harry M. Orlinsky (Philadelphia: The Jewish Publication Society of America, 1969).

11   *Kabbalah* (variously spelled *Kabalah, Cabalah, Cabala*) is the term for the mystic or esoteric teachings of Judaism concerning God and the universe. The principal book in kabbalistic literature is the *Zohar* (meaning "brightness"), dating back to thirteenth-century Spain. The classic reference on the subject is Gershom G. Scholem's *Major Trends in Jewish Mysticism* (New York: Schocken Books, 1941, 1946).

12   Stuart Gilbert's study, *James Joyce's Ulysses* (New York: Vintage Books, 1956), provides a detailed chart (p. 30) listing each of the episodes in *Ulysses,* together with its separate title, scene, associated color, organ of the body, etc. The chart is a kind of magnifying glass for those readers of Joyce who cannot spot the symbols with the naked eye.

13   The Joseph story in the Book of Genesis and Thomas Mann's great retelling of the story in his *Joseph and His Brothers* were the topics of the first series of conversations on the Bible between Mark Van Doren and Maurice Samuel. There were ten talks in all, which were broadcast on the national network of the National Broadcasting Company on "The Eternal Light" program of the Jewish Theological Seminary of America in the summer of 1953. The two saw multiple pits in the story: the one into which Joseph was thrown by his brothers; Egypt itself, into which he was sold in slavery; the prison where he was kept after the episode of Potiphar's wife; and again Egypt, into

which the children of Israel descended and were
ultimately enslaved.

14 King David ascended the throne of the United
Israelite Kingdom *ca.* 1005 B.C.E., and ruled until *ca.* 965 B.C.E. The first phase of the Babylonian
exile took place *ca.* 598–597 B.C.E. See chrono-
logical summary in *Ancient Israel* by Harry M.
Orlinsky (Ithaca: Cornell University Press,
1954), pp. 169–173.

15 The traditional Jewish view sees David not only
as the author of most of the psalms, but also as the
editor. The epilogue of a scroll found at Qumran
asserts that David had a library of 3,600 *tehillim*
(psalms) and 450 *shirim* (songs). Of the 150
psalms, seventy-three are ascribed to David; one
(Ps. 90) to Moses; two (Pss. 72 and 127) to Solomon; twelve (Pss. 50 and 73–83) to Asaph; one
(Ps. 88) to Heman the Ezrahite; one (Ps. 89) to
Ethan the Ezrahite (both Heman and Ethan were
leaders of the Temple musicians under David);
and eleven (Pss. 42, 44–49, 84–85, 87–88) to the
"sons of Korah" or the Korahites, thought to be
choristers during the days of the First Temple.
For a full discussion of the superscriptions, see
*E.J.*, vol. xiii, pp. 1317–1322.

16 Asaph was among the singers and musicians
named to major roles in the ceremonies connected with carrying the Ark up to Jerusalem (I
Chron. 15:17), and then he was appointed by
David to be chief of the Levites at the thanksgiv-

ing service (I Chron. 16:4ff.). Dr. Cohen in the
Soncino *Psalms* (p. 156) comments that Asaph
probably began the compilation of a hymnal
which was added to by his descendants, some of
them famous singers in the time of the Babylonian exile. (*See* Ezra 2:41.)

17   Sir Philip Sidney (1554–1586), English poet, soldier and statesman, was wounded in the thigh in
a skirmish connected with the battle of Zutphen
in the Netherlands, on July 22, 1586. As the story
goes, he was able to ride back to the British camp,
where he was supposed to have refused a cup of
water in favor of a dying soldier, saying, "Thy
need is greater than mine." He died at Arnheim
three months later and was mourned as a national
hero.

18   The legends honor Melchizedek as "the king of
righteousness, priest of God, and King of Jerusalem." He is supposed to have instructed
Abraham in the laws of the priesthood and in the
*Torah* (even though the *Torah* was not handed
down until Sinai). However, King Melchizedek
made the mistake of blessing Abraham first and
God second (*see* Gen. 14:19), for which "un-
seemly" lapse, God withdrew his "priestly dignity" and conferred it instead on Abraham. See
*Legends,* vol. i, pp. 233–234.

19   Judaism regards sex in marriage as good, proper,
and necessary for both wife and husband, and
thus this passage is somewhat perplexing. Hadas

translates v. 7 as: "I was, in truth, born with guilt,/ Conceived with sin ere I was born." The sense of the passage suggests that David was so abject and penitent about his sin with Bathsheba that he exaggerated: "I've been a sinner since the day I was born; no, since even before I was born!" The legends recounted in note 21 below hint that perhaps the legend-makers were also trying to explain v. 7.

20 The beautiful Abigail, one of David's principal wives, is discussed in *In the Beginning, Love* (esp. pp. 143–145).

21 The legends trace David's lineage to Miriam, the sister of Moses; the Book of Ruth tells the story of his great-grandparents, Ruth and Boaz. Jesse, David's father, is seen by the legend-makers as one of the greatest scholars of his day. But despite his piety, he was attracted to one of his female slaves, and only the intervention of his wife, called Nazbat in the legends, prevented him from siring an illegitimate son. Nazbat disguised herself as the slave, took the slave's place in Jesse's bed, and quite legitimately conceived and bore David. To keep up the pretense and to shield her husband from shame, Nazbat gave out that the boy was the son of the freed slave. See *Legends,* vol. iv, p. 82.

22 Dr. Cohen identifies "the river" as the Euphrates, the easternmost border that would have been known to the Psalmist. But vv. 8–11 extend over

the entire known world at the time. Soncino *Psalms*, p. 228.

23   Vergil's vision of a "just" Roman empire appears in the *Aeneid*, book vi, lines 851–853:

> Remember, O Roman, these shall be thy arts:
> To rule the nations with thy sway, to crown peace with law,
> To spare the humbled, and to tame in war the proud.

This was the basis of the *Pax Romana* which Augustus Caesar imposed on the world after the battle of Actium in 31 B.C.E., when he became the sole ruler of the Roman empire.

24   In *In the Beginning, Love* (esp. pp. 2–5).

25   Georg Wilhelm Hegel (1770–1831), quoted in George Bernard Shaw's *The Revolutionist's Handbook*.

26   The *Ashamnu* community confession expresses remorse for a multitude of sins in Hebrew alphabetical order: speaking slander, blaspheming, practicing deceit, acting arrogantly, wickedly, corruptly, etc. etc. A lucid translation appears in *The High Holyday Prayer Book*, translated and arranged by Ben Zion Bokser (New York: Hebrew Publishing Co., 1959), pp. 245, 270–271. Anyone who knows the Hebrew *alef bet* (alphabet) will recognize a number of other prayers with verses similarly written in Hebrew alphabetical order.

27  The legend-makers noted from the text of Num. 20:8 that God had instructed Moses to *speak* to the rock, and it would give out water. Instead, angered by the rebellious people, Moses struck the rock, not once but twice, whereupon God chided Moses for doubting His word. In the legends, the rock complains to God: "O Lord of the world! Why did Moses smite me?" Moses is then rebuked and later punished, for failing to judge the rock "in righteousness." *Legends,* vol. iii, pp. 319–320.

28  In the new translation of Ps. 137, the J.P.S. rendering of vv. 7–9 is very powerful:

*Remember, O Lord, against the Edomites the day of Jerusalem's fall;*
*how they cried, "Strip her, strip her to her very foundations!"*
*Fair Babylon, you predator, a blessing on him who repays you in kind what you have inflicted on us;*
*a blessing on him who seizes your babies and dashes them against the rocks!*

The Book of Psalms: *A New Translation according to the Traditional Hebrew Text (Philadelphia: The Jewish Publication Society of America, copyright 1972)*

29  Arnold J. Toynbee, *A Study of History,* I, 212n., quoted by Maurice Samuel in his book, *The Professor and the Fossil* (New York: Alfred A. Knopf, 1956), pp. 117–118.

30  Early Christians were accused by the Romans of killing babies for sacramental purposes. In the

Middle Ages, Christians turned the ghastly blood libel against the Jews. The first specific accusation came in Norwich, England, in 1144, when Jews were charged with murdering a boy named William for Passover ritual purposes. The libel spread throughout Europe. From the Middle Ages up to modern times, countless Jews were tried and massacred. The Nazis revived the libel; even after World War II, the Soviet Union was still circulating the lie as part of its anti-Israel and anti-Semitic campaign. See *E.J.,* vol. iv, pp. 1120–1131. Maurice Samuel's book, *Blood Accusation* (New York: Alfred A. Knopf, 1966) is the history of the Beiliss Case, the infamous trial of the Jew, Mendel Beiliss, falsely accused of a ritual murder in Czarist Russia, just before the Revolution.

In his beautiful, detailed history of the Passover *Haggadah,* titled *A Feast of History* (New York: Simon and Schuster, 1972), the British scholar Chaim Raphael describes the link between the ritual murder libel and the custom of reciting "Pour out Thy wrath . . ." at the Passover *seder.* See pp. 136–143.

31  Hadas translates the verse, "If I forget you, O Jerusalem,/May my right hand wither." The rabbinical commentators tell a chilling story about the Levitical musicians of the Temple who were dragged off into Babylonian exile, manacled and chained. Nebuchadnezzar ordered them to come and perform for him during his banquets, and to sing the Lord's song for him, as they had sung in

the Lord's Temple. Whereupon the Levites stood up, to a man, and mangled their playing thumbs. In reprisal, Nebuchadnezzar mounted a further slaughter of the captives. *Midrash,* vol. ii, pp. 334–335.

32   Exod. 16:31 likens manna to coriander seed, "white, and the taste of it was like wafers made with honey." Num. 11:7–8 elaborates: "The manna was like coriander seed, and the appearance thereof of the appearance of bdellium [thought to be a pearl or other similar precious stone]. . . . the taste was as the taste of cake baked with oil." The J.P.S. 1962 *Torah* translates the latter as: "It tasted like rich cream." Modern scholars suggest that manna may have been a lichen or a derivative of the tamarisk tree which grows to this day in the southern Sinai peninsula.

   The legends grow rapturous about the flavor and qualities of the manna. It was the "bread of the angels," and those who ate it became equal in strength to the angels. Its flavor was "miraculous." It required no cooking or baking, and the flavor varied from person to person. "To the little children," says *Legends,* "it tasted like milk, to the strong youths like bread, to the old men like honey, to the sick like barley steeped in oil and honey." Then *Legends* continues on to extol its marvelous delivery system and hygienic packaging:

*As miraculous as the taste of manna was its descent from heaven. First came a north wind to sweep the floor of the desert;*

*then a rain to wash it quite clean; then dew descended upon
it, which was congealed into a solid substance by the wind,
that it might serve as a table for the heaven descending manna,
and this frozen dew glistened and sparkled like gold. But, that
no insects or vermin might settle on the manna, the frozen dew
formed not only a tablecloth, but also a cover for the manna,
so that it lay enclosed there as in a casket, protected from
soiling or pollution above and below.*

Legends, *vol. iii, pp. 44–45.*

33   The Wisdom Books of the Bible were the theme
      of the ten-part series of conversations between
      Mark Van Doren and Maurice Samuel on "The
      Eternal Light" program on NBC radio in the
      summer of 1957.

34   C. S. Lewis, *The Screwtape Letters* (New York:
      Macmillan, 1959), p. 87.

35   Hadas translates "like a wineskin in the smoke"
      as ". . . I am like a shriveled wineskin." Soncino
      *Psalms* (p. 405) explains that wine used to be
      stored in animal skins, which in turn were stored
      in rooms without chimneys, and hence dried
      up.

36   Mark Van Doren wrote his master's thesis on
      Henry David Thoreau. It was later published, to
      wide acclaim. The passage referred to appears in
      Thoreau's *Walden; or Life in the Woods* (Garden
      City, N.Y.: Doubleday Anchor Books, 1973 edi-
      tion), p. 66.

37 "Bubble of dust"—R. L. Stevenson; "forked radish"—Shakespeare, *Henry IV;* and "two-legged animal"—Plato.

38 The J.P.S. 1962 *Torah* translates the Third Commandment: "You shall not swear falsely by the name of the Lord your God; for the Lord will not clear one who swears falsely by His name." Scholars, ancient and modern, have interpreted this commandment in a number of different ways. For an informed discussion, see Solomon Goldman's *The Ten Commandments,* ed. Maurice Samuel (Chicago: University of Chicago Press, 1956), pp. 152–160.

39 C. S. Lewis, *Reflections on the Psalms* (New York: Harcourt, Brace and Company, 1958), pp. 29–30.

40 Who is doing the "saying"—i.e., the cursing—the Psalmist or his adversaries? (Incidentally, the Hebrew for "adversary," or "accuser, persecutor" is *satan.*) In the original Hebrew, there is no punctuation, no capitalization, no separation of verses, adding to the already formidable problems of the translators. The *K.J.V.,* the *R.S.V.,* and the Smith translations omit the quotation marks at the beginning of v. 6, *Set Thou a wicked man over him. . . .* and at the close of v. 19; the J.P.S. 1972 *Psalms* and Hadas also omit the quotation marks. The effect of this, of course, is to make the Psalmist the curser. The 1917 J.P.S.

translation inserts the quotation marks. Commenting on this, Soncino *Psalms* observes (pp. 36, 37) that the "adversaries" (v. 4) are in the plural, while the curses in vv. 6–19 are directed against a single person. In v. 28, the Psalmist says, "Let *them* curse. . . ." Maurice Samuel and Mark Van Doren understand here that the Psalmist is *not* doing the cursing.

41    Robert Browning, "Instans Tyrannus," written in 1855. The complete poem may be found in *Selected Poetry of Robert Browning,* ed. Kenneth L. Knickerbocker (New York: The Modern Library, 1951), pp. 278–279.

42    Plutarch's *Life of Alexander* tells how the young ruler visited the old philosopher and inquired if he lacked anything, whereupon Diogenes replied, "Stand a little less between me and the sun."

43    Gerard Manley Hopkins (1844–1899), "Thou Art Indeed Just, Lord."

44    The numbering system of verses in the *K.J.V.* and *R.S.V.* is slightly different from that of the authorized Jewish versions. The "doorkeeper" image appears in Ps. 84:10 of both the *K.J.V.* and the *R.S.V.*

45    George D. Painter, *Proust: The Early Years* (Boston: Little, Brown and Company, 1959), p. xiii.

46 "Agenbite of Inwit" or "prick of conscience," the title of a fourteenth-century religious work, which James Joyce uses in *Ulysses* as a motif for the stings of guilt felt by Stephen Dedalus.

47 *Richard III,* act 1, scene 3.

48 Christopher Marlowe, *The Tragedy of Doctor Faustus,* scene 14. The clock has just struck eleven, and Faustus has only an hour left before the arrival of the Devil to claim his soul. Faustus calls out, *"O lente, lente . . . ,"* a quotation from Ovid, *Amores,* 1:13.

49 Dr. Johnson added one more touching detail in describing the incident to his friend, Henry White: the weather was very bad, and the old man stood bareheaded in the rain. *Boswell's Life of Johnson,* ed. with an introd. by Mowbray Morris (London: Macmillan and Co., 1929), p. 669.

50 The cheerful old gentleman was Mr. Edwards, "a decent-looking elderly man in gray clothes and a wig of many curls," who had been a classmate of Dr. Johnson's forty-nine years earlier at Pembroke College. In *Boswell's Life* (see note 49 above), pp. 472–473.

51 *The Confessions of St. Augustine* (London: J. M. Dent & Sons, 1939), pp. 25–26.

52 "Sin of Omission" by Mark Van Doren. It was first published in his *The Last Look and Other Poems*

(1937) and later included in his *Collected and New Poems, 1924–1963* (New York: Hill and Wang, 1963), pp. 206–207. Here it is quoted in full, by permission of Dorothy Van Doren:

### Sin of Omission

*He will remember this: the cunning Fates,*
*Seeing all seventy years laid flat ahead—*
*The spring-tight coil of days unrolls for them,*
*Their little and deep long eyes forewatch the dead—*
*The mouse-eyed Fates can number the known times*
*He will remember this, the thing unsaid.*

*Only to say it now would soothe that man*
*His father, come to sound him in his room;*
*Most friendly, but the stairs are still acreak,*
*And the boy, deafened to another doom,*
*Says nothing; he is guilty of desire*
*For the mind's silence, waiting to resume.*

*What it was filled with, he the least of all*
*In a far day will know; remembering then—*
*So the Fates reckon—how he ran and called,*
*Hoping to bring the shoulders up again;*
*But only called half-loudly in his pride,*
*And in the pride of him the best of men.*

*He will remember this, and loathe the hour*
*When his fair tongue, malingering, stood still.*
*He will rehearse the sentences not said;*
*Pretending that he climbed the lonely hill;*
*Pretending that he met him at the top,*
*Articulate, and cured him of his ill:*

*His need to know, so innocent, how sons*
*Read in their rooms the dark, the dear-bought books;*
*How in his own good flesh the strange thing grew,*
*Thought's inward river, nourishing deep nooks,*

*Dyeing them different-green. The boy will feign,*
*Concealing his long sighs, his backward looks—*

*Will fabricate warm deeds and laughing words,*
*His hand upon a chair, his cheeks alive;*
*Instead of this cool waiting, and this gloom*
*Wherein no starting syllable can thrive.*
*He will remember even as he runs.*
*The Fates run too, and rapider arrive.*

53   The J.P.S. 1962 *Torah* translation changed the
     old "Red Sea" of Exod. 15:4 to the "Sea of
     Reeds." The translation committee has explained
     (in *Notes on the New Translation,* p. 170, identified
     in note 10 above) that the Hebrew *yam suf* means
     "sea of reeds or rushes." *Suf* is borrowed from
     the Egyptian; the same word *suf* is found in Exod.
     2:3. The baby Moses was hidden among the suf
     along the bank of the river Nile. The *E.J.* conjec-
     tures several possible sites for the Sea of Reeds
     and offers maps to show the theoretical routes
     that the children of Israel may have taken in the
     Exodus from Egypt. See *E.J.,* vol. vi, pp. 1042–
     1050. Interestingly enough, one of the conjec-
     tured sites is the Bitter Lakes region, where the
     Israeli Army crossed over into Egypt in the Yom
     Kippur War of 1973. The *R.S.V.* of 1973 keeps
     to the old "Red Sea."

54   The musical rendition of the psalms in the Tem-
     ple is a fascinating and rich subject which curious
     readers may explore for themselves in numerous
     standard sources. One such source is *Jewish Music
     in Its Historical Development* by A. Z. Idelson (New
     York: Schocken Books, 1967). A second source

is the informative article, "The Jewish Contribution to Music" by Eric Werner in *The Jews: Their Role in Civilization,* ed. Louis Finkelstein (New York: Schocken Books, 1971, 4th ed.), chap. 4. Dr. Werner writes in part:

*In the simple solo psalmody, one person alone sings its prayer (Ps. 3–5). In the response psalm, the congregation answers the chanting soloist with short and concise formulae (Ps. 48, 100, 118). The antiphon has two groups chanting alternately (Ps. 136, 148), while in the refrain psalm a refrain verse is sung by a group and interjected into the singing of the full text, as rendered by a soloist (Ps. 135:1–3). . . .*

*Musical services are described in the passages of II Chron. 15:16–24; 16:4–7; 25:1–7, and the minute, meticulous organization of such services became the ideal of cult music for all Christianity. . . .*

*A contrafact is the use of a familiar melody for a new text. Thus, the anthem,* America (My Country, 'tis of Thee) *is a contrafact of the older* God Save the King; *. . . The use of the contrafact is probably as old as mankind, yet the first records of its being employed are found in the Psalms. Some of them bear superscriptions which have nothing whatever to do with their contents,* e.g. *Psalm 22, "To the chief musician upon the 'Hind of the Morning,' a psalm of David"; or Psalm 56, "To the chief musician upon 'Mute Dove far away' by David"; and so on. These odd superscriptions gave the first lines of folk songs, then familiar to the Psalmist. They indicated that the respective psalms were to be sung to particular tunes which, unhappily, have long since been lost.*

The Jews: *Vol. III:* Their Role in Civilization, *pp. 117–118.*

55 "On the *sheminith*" means literally "on the eighth" and may refer to an eight-stringed instru-

ment, according to the *E.J.,* vol. xiii, p. 1320.
The technical terms in the superscriptions are obscure today, just as they were already obscure two
thousand years ago at the time of the Second
Temple. The various guilds of singers and musicians apparently had their own terminology, and
they kept it such a professional secret from one
another that the exact meanings disappeared with
the guilds.

56  In *In the Beginning, Love,* pp. 24–26, the reader
will find an expansion on this idea of the "father
image."

57  *"Shiggaion"* or *"shiggayon,"* a term used in the
heading of Ps. 7. The *E.J.* links it to the Akkadian
word meaning "to howl, lament."

58  Maurice's last book was a hymn to Yiddish, which
he considered one of his three mother-tongues.
(The other two are English and Hebrew.) It is
called *In Praise of Yiddish* (Chicago: Henry Reg-
nery Co.—a Cowles book, 1971).

59  Hadas translates Ps. 116:15 as "Grievous in the
sight of the Lord/ Is the death of those who love
Him." The rabbinical commentators explained
this interpretation with a parable. A king sent his
officer to collect revenues due from a certain
man. The man hospitably lodged the officer for
ten days, and on each day voluntarily paid the
officer 10,000 shekels. At the end of the ten days,
the officer had received 100,000 shekels; but

upon checking the amount of assessment actually due, he discovered that the householder owed only fifty shekels. Whereupon the officer asked, "How can I presume to ask him for them?" Even so, the Lord lamented, "Grievous is it for Me to say to the righteous that they must die. Grievous was it for me to say to Abraham that he must die, seeing that he had proclaimed Me the Maker of heaven and earth . . . ," and equally grievous was it for Him to tell Isaac, Jacob, Moses, and David, all of whom had voluntarily performed far in excess of what had been due. Then the commentators added the "justification" for the deaths of the righteous: ". . . Because the righteous asked with their own mouths for death, the Holy One, blessed be He, said: Let these depart to make way for the others. Had Abraham gone on living, how could Isaac have come into authority? And Jacob? And Moses? And Joshua? And Samuel? And David and Solomon? . . ." *Midrash,* vol. ii, pp. 225–226.

60  "Statistically I am dead several times over," Maurice wrote in *Little Did I Know: Recollections and Reflections* (New York: Alfred A. Knopf, 1963). He calculated the odds, and observed, "However I look at it, I am astonished at being here." He was able to defy the statistics until his death, at the age of seventy-seven, in 1972.

61  The *R.S.V.* of 1973 appears to be the only major modern translation that retains the familiar "for ever." Smith translates the passage: "And I shall

dwell in the house of the Lord to an old age." The
J.P.S. 1972 *Psalms* uses "for many long years."
Hadas translates: "Throughout the long years
ahead/The Lord's house shall be my dwelling
place."

62  A paraphrase of a passage of Socrates' *Apology*
before the Athenian court, which Jowett translates: "Some one may wonder why I go about in
private giving advice. . . . I will tell you the reason
of this. You have often heard me speak of an
oracle or sign which comes to me, and is the
divinity which Meletus ridicules in the indictment. This sign I have had ever since I was a
child. The sign is a voice. . . ." *The Works of Plato,*
trans. into English and with analyses and intro-
ductions by B. Jowett (New York: Dial Press,
n.d.), pp. 120–121. Professor Milton Hindus of
Brandeis University was kind enough to check
the Greek texts of both Plato's *Apology* and of the
opening chapter of Xenophon's *Memorabilia* and
found the original word used, the first part of
which transliterates as *daimon,* although none of
the translations he consulted (Jowett and Fowler
for the Plato; Watson-Hughes for Xenophon)
used *daimon* in their English texts.

63  In my old copy of *The Thoughts of Marcus Aurelius
Antoninus,* trans. John Jackson (London: Hum-
phrey Milford, 1923), "Nature" with a capital N
appears too frequently to give any one reference.
Some samplings: "Universal substance is as wax
in the hands of universal Nature . . ." (Book vii,

23); "The time is all but come, when the Nature that administers the Whole shall transmute all that thou seest, using their substance for new creations . . ." (Book vii, 25); "Whether the universe is an aggregation of atoms, or a natural organism, let my first principle be that I am part of a whole governed by Nature . . ." (Book x, 6).

64  Matthew Fontaine Maury (1806–1873), an American naval officer and hydrographer who made important charts of the Atlantic Ocean. His book, *Physical Geography of the Sea* (1885), is regarded as the first classic of modern oceanography.

65  The bragging was muted by a warning against "cosmic impiety" by Russell in his *The History of Western Philosophy.* Maurice wrote about this, and about science and religion generally in his essay, "The Cultivation of Truthfulness," published posthumously, *Midstream* magazine, Aug.-Sept., 1973.

66  Benedict de Spinoza, "All excellent things are as difficult as they are rare." *Ethics,* Prop. XLII, Note.

67  Ben Jonson, *Discoveries, ca.* 1635: "I remember the players have often mentioned it as an honor to Shakespeare, that in his writing (whatsoever he penned) he never blotted out a line. My answer hath been, would he had blotted a thousand, which they thought a malevolent speech. I had

not told posterity this but for their ignorance,
who chose that circumstance to commend their
friend by, whereby he most faulted."

68 Sydney Smith, *Lectures on Moral Philosophy,* Lec-
ture 9 (1804).

69 See *Prince of the Ghetto* by Maurice Samuel (New
York: Alfred A. Knopf, 1948), pp. 205–208.

70 *To have dominion . . . .* In recent years, certain
ecology-minded Protestant scholars have conceived the notion that some biblical passages—
e.g., "and subdue it" and "have dominion" in
Gen. 1:28—are somehow to blame for giving
men license to despoil the earth. A group of Protestant theologians met at the School of Theology
in Claremont, Calif., in the spring of 1970 to
consider how traditional Christian attitudes,
derived from interpretations of Gen. 1:28, etc.,
had "given sanction" to the exploitation and
spoliation of natural resources. Earlier, an article
in *Science* magazine by Lynn White, Jr., a history
professor at UCLA, Los Angeles, had sounded a
similar note. Three years later, Arnold J. Toynbee was portentously, if somewhat belatedly,
echoing the same theme in an article in *Horizon*
(Summer '73) that was widely republished. However the Christian tradition may have interpreted
these biblical passages in the past centuries, the
Jewish tradition clearly has never understood the
Bible as giving any mandate to man for the rape

of our environment and resources or for the indiscriminate slaughter of animal life, or indeed, for hunting as a sport. To the contrary, Jewish tradition views man *not* as the owner of God's earth, but as the responsible caretaker. The Hebrew Bible is the source of such Jewish teachings as rest for domestic animals on the Sabbath, rest for the earth in the sabbatical year, and the concept of *tsa'ar ba'alay chayim,* the "pain of living creatures," or kindness to animals. For those who are interested, a concise summary of Jewish teachings about man's relationship to nature appears in the article by the distinguished Jewish scholar, Dr. Robert Gordis, "The Earth Is the Lord's: Judaism and the Spoliation of Nature," in *Keeping Posted* magazine, vol. xvi, no. 3, December, 1970), 838 Fifth Avenue, New York, N.Y. 10021.

An ancient rabbinical commentary on this theme has been translated by Jacob Sloan with the title, "Your World." It goes:

*In the hour when the Holy One, blessed be he, created the first man,*
*he took him and let him pass before all the trees of the garden of Eden,*
*and said to him:*
*See my works, how fine and excellent they are!*
*Now all that I have created for you have I created.*
*Think upon this, and do not corrupt and desolate my world;*
*for if you corrupt it, there is no one to set it right after you.*

*from* Hammer on the Rock: A Short Midrash Reader, *ed. Nahum N. Glatzer, trans. Jacob Sloan (New York: Schocken Books, 1948), p. 13.*

71   *R.S.V.* translates, "little less than God," and
Smith, "but little lower than God." J.P.S. 1972
*Psalms,* renders this, "little less than divine." The
Hadas version is, "You have made him almost
divine."

72   None of the commentators could offer any light
on the literal question, but *Midrash* provides a
dramatic expansion of the scene. As background
to this psalm, it should be remembered from II
Sam. 6 and I Chron. 15 that David brought the
Ark up to Jerusalem and placed it in a tent, since
there was not yet a Temple. According to the
tradition, David composed this Ps. 24 for this
glorious occasion. The *Midrash* picks up the story
a few decades later. Solomon is now king and he
is ready to place the Ark in its permanent home:

*You find that after Solomon built the Holy Temple, he sought
to bring the Ark into the Holy of Holies, but the gate was
strait: This gate was five cubits in height, and two and a half
cubits in width; the Ark was only a cubit and a half in length,
a cubit and a half in width, and a cubit and a half in height.
But cannot that which measures a cubit and a half be put in
a space that is two cubits and a half? But the truth is that
the gates held fast one to the other, and although Solomon cried
out twenty-four times, he was given no response. When he
said:* Lift up your heads, O ye gates *he received no response.
Again when he said:* Lift up your heads, O ye gates
. . . that the King of glory may enter *(Ps. 24:7) he received
no response. But when he said:* O Lord God, turn not away
the face of Thine anointed; remember the good deeds
of David Thy servant (II Chron. 6:42), *at that moment
the gates lifted up their heads, the Ark entered, and a fire came
down from heaven. (Why was Solomon put to such trouble?*

*Because he was arrogant. . . .)*

The Midrash on Psalms, *vol. i, pp. 343–344.*

73    In Jewish liturgy, Ps. 113–118 taken as a unit are
      called the *Hallel,* which is chanted in the syna-
      gogue on the major biblical festivals, and since
      1948 in many congregations, on Israel Indepen-
      dence Day as well. Tradition has it that Moses
      and the children of Israel recited the *Hallel* after
      the liberation from Egypt, and thus it has been
      included in the home ritual of the Passover *seder.*
      The Last Supper was the paschal meal, or the *seder*
      on Passover eve; if Jesus and his disciples were
      following the Jewish customs of the time, they
      would also have recited the *Hallel.*

74    The legends are half playful, half fearful about
      the great leviathan which God created on the fifth
      day to be His plaything and ruler over the sea
      animals. Leviathan is wonderful and awesome; his
      fins radiate such brilliant light that even the sun
      is obscured. On the fifth day, God created a mate
      for leviathan, but then had second thoughts: the
      pair might smother the earth! He therefore killed
      the female and pickled her, against the day when
      she and her mate would be served as the main
      course at the banquet for the righteous in the
      world-to-come. The great event will take place in
      tents made of leviathan's skin. Also on the menu
      at that heavenly feast will be *behemot,* the Great
      Ox, roasted; and *ziz,* the king of the birds, whose
      head reaches to the sky. The *ziz* once happened
      to lay a rotten egg, and carelessly discarded it.

Three hundred cedars were crushed, and sixty cities were flooded. *Legends,* vol. i, pp. 27–29.

75   The Rabbis of the *Talmud* took as their text the passage in Jer. 23:29, "Is not My word like . . . a hammer that breaketh the rock in pieces?" and went on to reason: "As the hammer splits the rock into many splinters, so will a scriptural verse yield many meanings." This was their way of saying that an infinitude of interpretations are possible as the result of the impact of God's word upon men's minds—all of them valid.

# INDEX